ALAN

THE EUREKA WAY

Navigating the financial advice
minefield without blowing your wealth

with Scott Francis and Fiona Harris

ABC
Books

Published by ABC Books for the
AUSTRALIAN BROADCASTING CORPORATION
GPO Box 9994 Sydney NSW 2001

First published in August 2007

ISBN 978 0 7333 2086 6.

Cover design by Nanette Backhouse at saso design
Set in 11/14 Sabon by Kirby Jones
Printed and bound in Australia by Griffin Press, Adelaide

5 4 3 2 1

CONTENTS

Chapter 1

DEFINING THE PROBLEM

Most of us find our brains go to mush when it comes to thinking about our finances. We may have confidence to have a go at running a business or teach classes — but when it comes to managing our money, we think we know our limitations. So millions of us serve ourselves up to an industry waiting eagerly to reassure us and to relieve us of our money: the financial services industry, particularly financial planners.

The stakes are very high indeed. Australians have almost $1 trillion (a million million dollars) sitting in superannuation funds these days and there's plenty more invested outside super as well, in property and shares. It's the era of self-reliance, of super choice and do-it-yourself (DIY) investing — of accumulation-type funds, which means how you will live in retirement depends on how well you invest your money while you are working.

Most of the money put aside by Australians for their retirement, or invested for income after retirement, passes through the hands of a financial planner or some other part of the financial services industry. This is virtually forced on us by the complexity of the savings system set up by the government. What's more, the government helps to create the illusion of safety through a massive regulatory infrastructure.

Yet this is an industry riddled with conflicts of interest created by sales commissions and 'unholy' relationships between advisers and the promoters of financial products. It is impossible to tell whether your adviser is acting in your best interests or simply selling you something.

This book sets out to explain how the financial services industry works and to help guide you through the challenges you may encounter in dealing with the financial planning industry. We are not against financial planning itself. In fact, we think nearly everyone should get advice at some time. But the advice should be better, more impartial, and cheaper.

Many financial planners are good at what they do and truly add value for their clients. The trouble lies not with individuals, but with the system. We are against a system designed to extract percentage fees from investors and seriously erode their savings in the process. This is highway robbery.

We believe the regulation of financial services in Australia is totally inadequate. Incompetent, conflicted, and sometimes corrupt, advisers are getting away with murder. And even if — by some miraculous regulatory intervention — the conflicts of interest from sales commissions could be removed, there are other more fundamental problems. The percentage fees charged for all financial services (not just financial planning) are too high and they are bleeding our retirement savings; and the service and expertise being provided for that money is patchy, unpredictable, and too often just plain bad.

Actually these are really just parts of one overriding problem: that the value for money of financial services is neither good enough nor reliable enough, and those of us who are getting help to save and plan for retirement, or who have already retired and need to live on their savings, are too often being badly served.

Retirement investment products are marketed with slick slogans and extravagant claims about a better tomorrow. But there is no tomorrow worth having for many who sign on to some of these so-called 'safe' investments. The disastrous Westpoint collapse of 2006 is no longer in the news, but we should never forget what happened and the thousands who lost everything because of bad advice.

In some ways, however, the danger of a big financial collapse is the least of our problems. The leaks, the small mistakes, the fees and the avoidable taxes are costing Australians millions every year. You may think that your financial plan is fine, but it is probably full of money leaks and excessive charges, as well as tax 'time-bombs' that won't explode until you go to withdraw income. And that's assuming you even *have* a financial plan which is not just a sales document that sells you entirely up the river.

Retirement saving is a 'game of inches', in which getting your fees and charges down by a few points can make a huge difference to your end result — the difference between spending much of your retirement in the Whitsundays sipping mint juleps, or just sitting miserably in your backyard watching your budget and sipping tea! Given that the returns are largely a matter of how the markets perform, and that most investment managers produce much the same results, the fees are the most important thing you can control.

But how often have you had a conversation with your financial planner about how to get your fees down? This should be the first priority of any financial adviser, yet all too often — in search of fraudulent illusory promises of higher returns — they simply ensure that your fees go up instead.

The stakes are enormous. Unfortunately, that's because we, the members of the current generation of savers and retirees, are the guineas pigs for a massive government experiment: the privatisation of retirement saving. The old era of company- or government-guaranteed retirement income has given way to a new era of enforced self-reliance — and although the sharemarket boom of the past three years and the added super tax benefits in this year's budget, has made the whole thing seem like a soda — it's not.

Retirement is one of the most complicated jobs you'll ever undertake; a constant battle against hidden fees, higher taxes, rising inflation and complicated investment products. The shift to self-reliance has become necessary because of the ageing of the Australian population. It's probably a good thing, but even that can't be taken for granted, especially if we end up going through a bad time on investment markets. The past few years have been fantastic for investors in Australia, but how long can it last?

There are two reasons why responsibility for retirement saving has been forced upon us by corporations and governments. It isn't just because of the ageing of the population and the extra financial burden of growing numbers of retirees. It's also because corporations and governments no longer want to bear the market risk inherent in guaranteeing employees with a certain standard of living in retirement. This trend started after the oil shocks of the 1970s, which produced a once-in-a-generation spike in inflation and then interest rates, with subsequent inevitable market volatility.

Before the end of the 1980s, boards of directors and government cabinets were making plans to shift market exposure back to employees. As it happens, this has coincided with an unprecedented period of prosperity and stability — a bull market — which has lasted for 16 years (accelerating in the past three years, after a pause following the internet bust).

But those of us suddenly burdened with responsibility of worrying about our retirement are surprisingly happy about things. We're doing better than we would have with corporate and government super (except, of course, unless you are a judge or politician; their arrangements were — and usually still are — fabulous).

The trouble is that the bull market has covered up a rotten core in the system set up to help us with that money. It has grown up as a minefield of conflicts of interest and hard-sell (disguised as advice) by which you can be robbed blind without even noticing it, because the returns look pretty good, thanks to the rising tide of the markets.

It's a system designed for the financial health of the businesses selling products, not yours.

We believe future generations will have better choices and that the advice industry will have more integrity and tougher regulation. A future chairman of ASIC will do more than just suggest that the industry should regulate itself. They will actually take a stick to those who are selling products on commission while pretending to give unbiased advice. A new system of designation, in which advice and sales are clearly separated, will be introduced. Those 'advisers' who are relying on those two things being mixed up will suffer and consumers will get a fair deal.

Our children and grandchildren will be able to rely on a new breed of financial planner, one with years of specialised education and advanced qualifications, who charges a reasonable fee for the service provided and doesn't skim a percentage off the top forever. When you move to a new town or suburb, you'll simply be able to turn up at the local financial planner and know you'll be dealing with someone with integrity and expertise, who won't sell you a prescription for wealth on commission.

In fact, financial planners should be (and one day will be) like wise and ethical doctors. Future planners will diagnose retirement planning problems and prescribe precise and effective solutions in the same way doctors prescribe drugs — uncorrupted by sales commissions from drug companies.

But for the moment you have to get by with the current varied collection of planners, brokers, bankers and salesmen who are each trying to get a piece of your retirement money for themselves. Some are really good, most are ordinary and some are downright bad. On the whole, getting good, independent financial advice can be a tall order.

Since we set up the Eureka Report, an independent online publication providing investors with a cost-effective source of in-depth analysis and investment education, one of the most common questions we get asked is: 'Where can I find good, independent financial advice?' That's why we have now gone one step further with The Eureka Way, a new website that lists independent fee-for-service advisers who don't take commissions. (www.theeurekaway.com.au) The Eureka Way also provides a second opinion on financial plans.

Although many industries are influenced by sales commissions and conflicts of interest, this problem is worst of all in the financial planning industry because the stakes are so high and because there's a big gap between perception and reality, between what we think the financial planners do and what they are really doing.

Many of us think financial planning is simply a service designed to help us reach our personal and lifestyle goals by protecting and growing our wealth. That is, by employing a financial planner to guide us through the maze of products and investment noise, we should be able to save in the way that's most likely to meet our needs and even stick to an investment strategy when the market tests our patience.

But that's not what the industry was set up for.

While the financial planning industry is changing and improving, it was initially designed as a system for selling. Financial planners distribute products from fund managers, banks and insurance institutions. They are just salespeople for the financial services industry.

The trouble, in our view, is that they portray themselves as something akin to doctors — financial health consultants — not as salespeople. The system of commissions they use is no different to any other sales profession. The manufacturers of financial products (the banks, funds management groups and insurance institutions) pay commissions to sell their products and to sell lots of them.

What this means for you, the investor, is that the financial advice you receive is tainted. Sometimes it is not, but often the advice you get is not motivated solely by the desire to best serve your interests. It's more likely to be motivated by a desire to sell. If a financial planner has a routine choice between recommending a product that pays them a higher commission over another, which one would they most likely choose? Remember that most investors do not question their advisor's motivation, and also never forget that financial planners have their own family and lifestyle to consider.

In addition to the issue of motives, the ownership structure within the financial services industry needs to be made explicit. Many of the institutions that make financial products and pay the commissions actually also own a large number of financial planning businesses! So there are conflicts within conflicts.

This means institutions can manufacture products and then distribute them through a tied network of distribution. For example, ANZ Bank owns ING, one of Australia's largest fund managers and life insurers, and ING owns several distribution networks, namely Tandem, Millennium 3, RetireInvest and ING Financial Planning.

Other examples include the Commonwealth Bank, which owns the dealer group, Financial Wisdom; financial services monolith AMP owns AMP Financial Planning, Hillross and Arrive Wealth Management; Godfrey Pembroke, Apogee Financial Planning, Garvan, MLC Financial Planning and

National Australia Financial Planning are all subsidiaries of National Australia Bank's wealth-management arm MLC.

While some of these groups, particularly MLC, have made significant inroads into reducing bias and conflicts within its business models by moving to a fee-for-service model, the ownership structure is well entrenched in the financial services industry, so that financial planners remain product distributors.

The benefit of a tied distribution structure for product manufacturers is that it allows them to exert further influence over the type and range of products their distribution network offers its customers. They usually construct the approved product lists or investment menus from which their planners offer their clients products and platforms, so they have influence over the inflows particular products receive.

Thus your best interests are pushed even further down the list of priorities by such close relationships between product manufacturers and distribution. It's often pretty safe to conclude that your interests are way down the bottom of the priority stack.

It is in this system, where distribution is king, that product manufacturers will and do pay virtually anything to have their products listed on financial planner's product menus. For example, a wrap (master trust) operator called Asgard recently started charging other fund managers $200,000 to become a 'preferred partner'; that is, to have their products listed on Asgard's investment platform, which gives the other fund managers access to some 900 financial planners and their clients.

Financial planning is part of a financial services industry worth billions of dollars. The Investment and Financial Services Association (IFSA), which represents the retail and wholesale funds management industries, estimates that its members invest more than $950 billion on behalf of over nine million Australians and earn at least $2 billion for doing so.

It's little wonder the industry is a bit reluctant to change a structure that has served it so well. In fact, it has an uncanny ability to invent new ways of extracting even more fees from investors. One of these extraction devices is known as 'platforms and wraps', which will be dealt with in more detail later in this book.

More than 80 per cent of retail funds are now invested via a platform product known as wraps or master trusts. These products are administration vehicles that make it easier for financial planners to manage clients' accounts. However, they have introduced a whole new tier of fees for the investor, eroding any cost saving they may make by accessing wholesale funds.

The Australian financial services industry and its regulation is in a state of constant change, especially after the introduction of the *Financial Services Reform Act 2001* (*FSRA*). This legislation covers compliance, disclosure, licensing and training regulations. It has raised the bar in terms of qualification of financial advisers and stamping out some of the less 'savoury' practices, such as 'soft dollar' remuneration, where planners were rewarded with overseas trips for high-volume sales.

However, the *FSRA* reforms only fully came into effect in 2004 and they are, to put it mildly, imperfect. Yes, the law now requires a lot more disclosure, but the paperwork has become so voluminous that financial planning clients are less likely than before to read it. Unless a planner clearly tells a client what sales commissions he or she is getting, and what effect commission has on their recommendations, the client is unlikely to find out.

Some planners do this. These days more and more planners are spurning commissions and working for a fee-for-service only, but it's entirely voluntary and ad hoc. It means you can never be sure whether the financial planner you visit is one of the 'good guys', or someone who seems nice but is really just pushing you into a financial product that pays them the best commission.

Two years after financial services reforms, we're still seeing the fallout of a tighter regulatory regime, with a fairly constant stream of bans against individual planners and survey results that show many financial planners are not acting in their clients' best interests.

In fact, one of the largest and most respected financial planning networks, AMP, has been operating under an enforceable undertaking imposed by industry regulator, the Australian Securities & Investments Commission (ASIC), to improve its compliance and disclosure practices.

The Financial Planning Association of Australia, the industry's peak professional organisation representing about 12,000 financial planners, has also put structures in place to increase professional standards within the industry, most notably its Code of Ethics and Rules of Professional Conduct, which set strict guidelines for its members.

Now investors are becoming more financially literate and aware of the complexity of the financial services industry, many are turning to DIY investing to seize control of their own affairs. In fact, DIY investing is the largest growth area for the financial services industry, best demonstrated by the growth of DIY superannuation vehicles known as self-managed superannuation funds or SMSFs.

According to the Australian Prudential Regulation Authority (APRA), as at June 2006 SMSFs accounted for 23 per cent of total superannuation assets, second only to retail funds with just over 32 per cent.

Wealth creation through DIY investing is a good option. By investing in growth assets, using tax-effective vehicles, such as superannuation, and managing your expectations, DIY investing can be a rewarding experience. Good advice has a role to play in DIY investing as well.

Chapter 2

HOW FINANCIAL PLANNING WORKS

We have all heard stories about life insurance endowment products that were worth less at the end than when they started because of excessive fees and commissions.

That's how super began life. Retail investment products (as we now know them) evolved out of life insurance policies, which used to be sold with undisclosed fees and commissions that were so big it was virtually impossible for customers to end up ahead. Nevertheless insurance companies and their agents became very rich indeed.

The insurance agents who collected those secret sales commissions have now changed their names to 'financial planners'. They sell managed funds and superannuation — similar products, same distribution system, but with different names. And thwarting most attempts to better protect consumers in financial services is the fact the products they sell came with them out of life insurance, with its appalling history of secret commissions and rip-offs.

The spin involved in using the terms 'financial planner' and 'financial adviser', rather than simply changing the label 'insurance agent' to 'investment agent', has meant that consumers think they are getting something more than product sales; they think they are getting independent, disinterested advice.

The industry is beginning to change as financial planners realise they are heading up a dead-end street of low consumer esteem and accountants get licences to become financial planners, bringing with them their charge-by-the-hour culture. A lot of the time, accountants making the switch to financial planning think 'Wow! How long has this been going on?' before they join in the lucrative sales commission party.

The retail financial services industry is evolving rapidly, but not necessarily in a particularly healthy direction. Financial planners used to just sell their employers' products; these days the business is more like supermarket shopping. Arguing about whether AMP or AXA or a bank-owned financial planning network is pushing clients into their own 'home brand' managed funds in return for commissions is fighting yesterday's battle. No longer about favouring particular managed funds, these days it's all about 'platforms', also known as 'wraps' or 'master trusts'. (Which are very similar to supermarkets in many ways.) Platforms and wraps are pivotal, so we have devoted an entire chapter to them (see Chapter 6).

AMP chief executive Andrew Mohl pointed out that AMP's platforms move clients' funds into a variety of managed funds owned by a wide range of fund managers, large and small, many of whom are competitors of AMP. So when you go to an AMP financial planner, you are shopping for a variety of branded managed funds, including AMP's 'home brand', at an AMP 'supermarket'.

These days commissions paid to financial planners are not designed to favour particular managed fund products, but to compensate the financial planner for the sales 'advice' provided to the client. The planner simply gets a cut out of the platform fees, but in most cases that cut makes no difference to which platform the client's money is put on: planners are generally tied to their licence holders and their proprietary platforms and they would use it anyway.

Even independent planners generally only use one platform, so the commissions they receive make no difference on a day-to-day basis (although they undoubtedly influence the decision about which platform to go with).

So what's the problem with the planner's cut from the platform? After all, the planner has to make a living and people have to be pushed to save more than the basic 9 per cent of their salary. If you hit a client with a $2–4000 invoice up-front, they might simply walk out of the office and not get the advice they need. It is far better, industry leaders and supporters often suggest, to deceive them into thinking they are getting the advice for nothing, so at least they get advice.

There are three problems with the platform fees that are paid to financial planners these days:

1 The payment of platform fees is controlled by the licence holder (bank or financial services company), which uses them to encourage sales through volume bonuses.
2 The 'advice' the commissions pay for is patchy, inconsistent and very often entirely worthless.
3 The commissions are often financed by 'shelf fees' charged by platforms to fund managers to be listed, in much the same way as supermarkets charge certain manufacturers to have their grocery items on their shelves.

On point one, commissions are not simply an equal, more palatable, alternative to fees-for-service. That's because they are controlled by the suppliers of the products. A fee-for-service can be deducted from a client's account in the same way as a commission, so it is not a $2–4000 bill up-front, but at least it is controlled by the client and not the platform owner.

This is where the supermarket analogy breaks down. For a start, supermarkets don't charge an entry fee, and they certainly don't charge you a percentage of your weekly grocery bill on top of the margin they get on the groceries.

But more fundamentally, customers don't go to financial planners to go shopping, they go for *advice*.

Some people know that if they go to a financial planner they are, in fact, walking into an investment supermarket, but most don't. In any case, financial planning networks promote their advice, not the shopping experience, as Coles and Woolworths do. Clients are encouraged to think they are going to see someone who can help them with their financial affairs, not to a financial supermarket.

And some people understand before they get there that, for example, Hillross, Arrive Wealth Management, Magnify Financial Planners and PremierOne are all part of the AMP 'supermarket chain', but most people have no idea.

In the end, despite all these fundamental flaws, it comes down to the quality of the advice you receive and, in fact, whether you are given advice at all, as opposed to a sales job, from a person who doesn't *seem* to be a salesperson.

Financial advisers are not all the same. They are not even all as good as each other. In fact, the quality drops away pretty quickly. Truth is, it is not very difficult to get a financial planning licence. Most of the knowledge is about the products for sale, rather than academic or astute questions of finance and investment.

Some financial planners are people we would willingly entrust with our money — professionals who are experts in a range of financial matters and have integrity. Many are not. Sorting the wheat from the chaff is not easy and financial planning network owners, banks and other financial services companies certainly won't tell us.

Quite often, even from the good planners, the 'advice' is just a sales job: the planner advises the client to move their money from one fund to another, or, more specifically, from an industry super fund to the planner's own master trust, from which he or she gets a commission.

Finally, platforms are not unbiased purveyors of managed funds: sometimes they charge fees to funds to be included on their list. Financial planners tell clients they are looking after their interests and presenting a selection of the most suitable funds for them to invest in. But this is, in many cases, simply a lie. They present a range of funds that are paying their shelf fees. This has very little to do with the best interests of the client.

Platforms and super funds should only ever choose funds that are going to provide the best investment returns for clients. That they clearly don't makes us wonder about the value of the advice promoted so assiduously by the industry. After all, this is the entire competitive proposition of their business: that they offer advice and industry super funds do not.

How is the financial planning industry structured?

About 18,000 planners make up the Australian financial planning industry. Of this number, about 14,000 are part of a dealer group, a large network of financial planners who work under the one Australian Financial Services Licence (AFSL). Typically, dealer groups are owned by large institutions, but this is not always the case.

According to the 2005–06 'Money Management Top 100 Dealer Group' survey, the two largest dealer groups in the financial planning industry are Professional Investment Services (with more than 1329 financial planners) and AMP Financial Planning (with 1259 planners).

The dealer group structure adds another layer of complexity to the financial planning industry and gives even more reasons to understand and question the motivation behind advice given by a financial planner.

The dealer group–planner relationship works in two ways.

- From a product manufacturer's point of view, a dealer group provides a ready-made distribution channel for their products. As the licensees, they can assemble an approved product list from which their planners select products, thereby exerting influence over which products make it to the list and which are excluded. In doing so, they can distort the demand for particular products and promote their own in-house products by making sure they have a guaranteed spot on the investment menu. It's like going to a particular car dealership and expecting to be shown all cars. It just doesn't happen.
- From a financial planner's perspective, the dealer group model is also attractive. Planners and their businesses can tap into the economies-of-scale of a larger institution, as well as utilising the resources made available to them by the licensee. Apart from assisting with the licensing costs, a licensee will also provide generous business support to help financial planning businesses meet their compliance and disclosure requirements, as well as back-office support, such as marketing materials and administration.

These benefits are particularly attractive to financial planners, more so since the inception of the *FSRA* regime, which, planners say, has given them more paperwork than ever before. They argue that meeting the new disclosure and compliance standards has increased their business costs and eroded the amount of time they can spend with their clients.

Given the distribution potential a dealer group can offer a product manufacturer, it is not uncommon for a financial institution to own several dealer groups. For example ING, the large funds-management and insurance business, owns four dealer groups: Tandem, Millennium 3, RetireInvest and ING Financial Planning. Having multiple dealer groups gives ING greater control and influence in distributing its products, as well as the opportunity to build ongoing relationships with a larger number of investors.

Since most dealer groups do not share the same name as their parent institution, it's difficult for investors to identify links between financial planning businesses and parent institutions. This information must be disclosed in a Financial Services Guide, a document that must be given to investors prior to their doing business with an institution. It discloses information regarding ownership structures, services and fee information.

Although dealer groups have common owners, they each have their own target markets, service and value propositions, approved product lists and fee structures. There is no consistency in service across the dealer groups, which creates greater confusion for anyone trying to find and use a financial planner.

Why is the industry structured like this?

The financial advice industry was always structured around selling products, and for many years this was accepted as a valid role. In some ways, even today its sales function is not regarded as a bad thing, as long as investors know why a financial planner could be promoting a particular product or platform.

In Australia, the financial advice industry is relatively young. It all began in the mid-1980s when the Australian financial services industry experienced tremendous growth. The deregulation of the financial system, together with an explosion in the range and number of products on offer, created a greater need for financial advice.

At the time, there was no formal financial planning industry. Insurance agents were the closest thing to financial advisers, offering investors advice while they sold life insurance and earning healthy commissions in the process.

With the introduction of compulsory superannuation in 1992, the Australian financial services industry saw an opportunity to broaden its advice base and 'sell' all types of financial products, and thus secure a viable future. As more money was invested and the funds management industry rapidly expanded and became more competitive, the manufacturers of financial products needed to establish formal distribution networks to sell their products.

So they beefed up their existing distribution networks, based on the old life insurance sales networks. No qualifications were needed. New recruits were simply offered in-house training on all of the parent company's products. Problems in the 1990s with agents mis-selling products and over-promising on investment returns soon made it obvious this bourgeoning industry needed greater regulation.

Reform of the financial services industry finally came in the form of the *Financial Services Reform Act 2001* (*FSRA*) — the most far-reaching reform legislation the Australian financial service industry has experienced. This legislation included regulation of the education and training of financial planners as well as disclosure and compliance requirements, although it did not come into full effect until 2004.

Today we continue to see fallout from an industry clambering to meet the new regulation requirements. The question remains: can all of this regulation solve the inherent conflicts of interest in the financial planning industry? To provide a simple recommendation for a client, which has to be recommended within a 'Statement of Advice', masses of paperwork must be completed. Contrast this with a trip to the doctor, where a GP can give a recommendation in 15 minutes, based on nothing more than the GP's professional judgement, accrued through many years of gruelling study leading to a medical degree.

Financial planners deal with issues of money rather than health, but arguably they are just as important. GPs, as professionals, stand for much of what is missing in the financial services industry. They are extremely well trained, independent of any products that they recommend and paid a reasonable fee for the time they spend assessing and treating the patient.

By contrast, financial planners possess varying types and amounts (sometimes cursory) of training, and they receive sales commissions from the products they 'prescribe'. They often earn unreasonably large incomes, and receive big retirement payouts when they sell their practices.

As it stands the industry is a minefield for consumers. But there is hope! The best defence is to learn about it, which is where we come in.

Commissions

Time and again surveillance campaigns conducted by the industry's regulator, the Australian Securities & Investments Commission (ASIC), prove that financial planners are motivated and corrupted by commissions.

The financial planning industry is a complex structure designed by product manufacturers to enable them to exert influence over the behaviour and businesses of financial planners for their own benefit.

Why do financial planners hold such sway in the financial services industry? Power brokers in the wider financial services industry try and influence them. They have the most important relationship in the whole financial services industry: they have direct contact with you, the investor.

Big money is involved and the stakes are very high. As mentioned in Chapter 1, the Investment and Financial Services Association (IFSA), which represents the retail and wholesale funds management industries, estimates its members invest in excess of $950 billion on behalf of more than nine million Australians.

With compulsory superannuation providing a solid platform of reliable funds for the Australian financial services industry, these figures are always on the rise. For example, the Australian Prudential Regulation Authority (APRA) estimated that total superannuation assets had increased by 19.8 per cent during 2005–06, to $913.9 billion. That means fees are growing by the same percentage. Nice work if you can get it: inflation is 3 per cent and GDP growth is about the same, but the gross income of the industry that is servicing Australia's superannuation pool is growing by close to 20 per cent per annum, without its members doing more than skimming.

In December 2006 we saw these superannuation savings exceed $1 trillion, thanks to continued strong investment returns and the ongoing 9 per cent compulsory employer superannuation contributions. With such a reliable source of funds, the Australian financial services industry is like a self-feeding beast, driven mainly by the 9 per cent compulsory super, but also by a complex system that validates the need for financial advice and a business structure built on maximising funds under management.

Along with the complexity of the structure of the industry is the reality that the majority of the public's financial education is provided by the financial services industry itself. Not surprisingly, much of this so-called 'education' fails to question the shortcomings of the industry. This sounds like getting rid of the doctors and letting the drug company reps diagnose *and* sell drugs to the patients. This leaves people believing myths that support the industry: that managed funds are the best solution for all; that wraps are the only way to take care of the administration of your portfolio; that past performance allows us to predict future performance; and, the myth perhaps most widely held, that financial planning is too hard and should be left to financial planners. Such notions are not worthy of a sophisticated country and these simplistic ideas are challenged throughout this book.

The financial planning industry was originally designed to sell financial products through the provision of advice. It was, and still is, called 'advice-based distribution'. If you understand that, and fully consider the implications of it, you will be most of the way towards understanding what financial planning is, and what's wrong with it.

Most of the financial advice industry today remains as a distribution arm for the makers and promoters of lucrative financial products: mainly banks, fund management groups and insurance companies.

These institutions make and sell financial products designed to attract your savings and to build the funds under management, on which they collect fees and therefore build profits.

When you make an appointment with a financial planner, the planner is required to ask many personal and financial questions so they can understand your needs and goals and match them with a strategy designed to help you reach your goals.

Under the regulations, the official aim of the exercise is to select the right products to suit the client's strategy. Note that it's all about the platforms and products to be chosen, not the investment strategy itself. Most financial planners work from an approved product list, a menu of products assembled by the institution with whom they are licensed to provide advice. But that's not the end of it: licensed financial planners can and sometimes do go outside the recommended list when an especially high sales commission beckons.

That's what happened with Westpoint. It still happens with managed investment schemes, such as timber plantations, that pay up-front commissions to the financial planner of 10 per cent. Yes, you read right — 10 per cent, of the clients' funds go to the person who suggested you buy.

Even within the recommended lists, mainstream investment product manufacturers (as they are called in the industry) *pay financial planners excessive commissions on an up-front and/or ongoing basis as a reward for choosing their product.*

That means when you invest in a financial product (a managed fund or life insurance) a percentage of your initial investment goes directly to a financial planner. For example, if an investment product (these days mainly platforms or master trusts) has an up-front commission of 5 per cent and your investment is $100,000, unless a financial planner chooses to rebate this fee or 'dial down' the amount (yes, they can do that), they will take $5000 of your initial investment and you will actually be investing $95,000.

It's even worse with ongoing, or 'trailing' commissions, which are calculated as a percentage of the total amount invested over the lifetime of the investment. It means a financial planner will continue to earn a nice little income over the course of the investment, no matter what.

The average trailing commission is about 0.6 per cent per annum, which really adds up over time. A survey conducted by *Choice* magazine in 2005 found trailing commissions range from 0.25 to 0.88 per cent. This is why an increasing number of financial planners and discount managed fund brokers will offer clients 'nil up-front fees' for managed fund investments — they want to collect the ongoing trailing commission for as long as the investment remains in place!

In many cases, up-front and trailing commissions are earned irrespective of the service given by a financial planner or a product's performance. This is an important point, and one that should not be overlooked. In a *Choice* article entitled 'Trail Commissions, Money for Old Jam', research from a 2004 Financial Planning Association survey was quoted, showing that 49 per cent of the 129 financial planning products were not reviewed annually.

So the first and most important thing to understand about the financial planning industry is that it is sales-driven and like most people in sales, most financial planners are paid commissions.

This may come as news to those who thought an industry that has the name 'advice' and is apparently designed to provide a personalised service, and which is supposed to take the time to get to know our lifestyle goals, would in fact be acting in our best interests.

This is sometimes, but not always, the case and it is the most profound deception perpetrated by the financial planning industry. When we walk into a travel agent to buy a holiday, for example, we know that they are paid through commissions, so we understand their vested interest in selling to us. In fact, we have specifically gone there to buy something. With the financial advice business it's different: most customers are looking for advice, they're not just interested in buying something. It's an industry in which the sales process is disguised.

RMIT University adjunct professor in financial planning Wes McMaster noted, 'One of the hallmarks of a true profession is that the professional is paid by the client, not a product provider. Imagine if doctors were paid by drug companies for the advice they give.'

This is perhaps the ugliest side of the financial planning industry because while a commission structure exists, there will always be the question of whether financial planners are acting in our best interests or their own desire to maximise their commission payments.

But there's more. The commission structure is just the first and worst conflict of interest in the financial planning industry. Further conflicts involve the way approved products lists are constructed and the dominant authority of the dealer group structure — including arrangements for buying their financial planners' practices when they retire.

Buyer of last resort

Financial planners are like most people in small business. They usually work hard and draw a salary — usually a minimal one — with the idea of building something of value that they can sell to finance their own retirement. For many, it's all about building the value of the business.

Underpinning this, and therefore the financial planning industry as a whole, is what's called the 'buyer of last resort' facility. This is the commercial arrangement that ties a financial planning practice to an investment product manufacturer, usually a bank or life insurance company. The bank agrees to buy the business at an agreed multiple of the ongoing commission income the planner has managed to build up.

They call it 'a multiple of recurring revenue' (not commissions), but we know what they mean. It is revenue that recurs every year, whatever happens. That is, trailing commissions on the product or percentage-based platform fees. Same thing.

Moreover, many banks pay a higher multiple on 'recurring revenue' from their own products. The standard formula for valuing a financial planning practice is three times recurring revenue. Many banks and wealth management companies, however, pay a multiple of four times revenue from their own investment funds and wrap accounts.

Some financial planning network owners have begun to introduce score-based systems, where the financial planning practice is valued according to a point system, with points awarded on a variety of quantitative and qualitative measures, including client satisfaction and quality of advice.

But the basis of the system remains three times revenue from external products and four times revenue from internal products for most firms.

Most financial planners are good, honest people trying to do the right thing by their clients and by themselves and their families. But no matter how 'good' a person may be, everybody responds to financial stimuli. Pay a chief executive according to earnings per share and he'll recommend a share buyback to get the earnings per share up; reward a stockbroker according to the number of transactions he books and he'll recommend his clients to trade shares every day if he can.

Reward a financial planner for the amount of trailing commission they build up, then they will build up a lot of trailing commissions. Make it an even bigger reward for certain products, then that's what will be sold.

This is why the move towards hourly fees in the provision of financial advice is so slow: it is not valued as highly and there is no mechanism to easily value that revenue.

A traditional accounting practice, where all revenue is from hourly, invoiced fees, is typically sold at a discount to gross revenue of about 20 per cent. That is, practices are usually sold for about 80 cents in the dollar of 'maintainable' billings. Financial planning practices are sold for three or four times that figure.

No wonder so many accountants are deciding to become financial planners! They can have the same number of clients and work just as hard, but end up selling their business for up to 400 per cent of gross revenue instead of 80 per cent of gross revenue.

Many banks dangle a further carrot in front of their financial planners: a 20 basis point (0.2 per cent) 'override' when their 'funds under advice' hits $100 million. That means the difference between having clients with assets of $99 million and $100 million is an extra profit of $200,000 a year, and three times that as a lump sum on retirement.

That's why there is such hot demand for financial practices at the moment. Advisers are desperate to build their funds under advice and get that extra 0.2 per cent by buying an established business. Brokers say they get scores of inquiries, and many genuine buyers, for every advice business that comes on the market.

Accounting firms, by comparison, are not scaleable: each accountant's income, and the value of his or her practice, is limited by the number of hours in the day, or rather by the number they can bill. A financial planning practice, by contrast, can build up huge levels of 'FUM' (funds under management) by just putting on extra staff and finding richer clients.

The 'buyer of last resort' facility is an important blockage to industry reform because banks and other 'manufacturers' use it to manipulate financial planners into pushing their own products. Until it changes, financial planners who are connected to a bank or life insurance company will not recommend the full range of investment products, such as direct shares, property, cash, and so on, even if those choices are the most appropriate for clients.

Disclosure

The result of all this is a lethal combination of factors, which make it very hard to challenge the status quo. Yet despite the challenges and the vested interests, the financial planning industry, and the financial services industry more generally, are slowly becoming more transparent.

Reforms introduced under the *Financial Services Reform Act 2001 (FRSA)*, which came into effect in 2002 with a two-year transitionary period, made it mandatory for financial planners to disclose their fees and commission structures in documents known as Financial Services Guides and Product Disclosure Statements.

Many in the industry argue that as long as the investor understands they are paying commissions and they are given a choice in the way they remunerate their planner, there is nothing dishonest about the system. But, as mentioned earlier, while commissions are paid there will always be a question about whether the client's best interests are being served and the integrity of the industry.

Anyway, it is quite possible to have too much disclosure. These days the combination of the statutory Statement of Advice, the Financial Services Guide and the Product Disclosure Statement, often running into hundreds of pages, is simply too much. As a result the *FSRA* has become a mechanism for concealment rather than disclosure, because clients don't read all the bumf.

Under the *FSRA* reforms, financial planners must demonstrate adherence to the 'know your client' and 'know your product' rules. These basically mean financial planners must know and understand their clients' needs and match these with the most suitable financial products. But the rules do not spell out that planners must act in their clients' best interests.

An advisory business has legal obligations to give personal advice that suits clients' needs; to take legal responsibility for its staff and representatives; to act efficiently, honestly and fairly and, finally, to meet standards that are designed to protect you against anything going wrong.

Independence

Beyond the dealer group structure described earlier, there are financial planning businesses that operate free from product restrictions and ownership links. But they are a minority, considering that there are only approximately 4000 financial planners who are not part of a dealer group network. Some of these businesses operate on a fee-for-service basis. This means you pay by the hour, so their remuneration is not tied to up-front or trailing commissions.

Given that they are a minority business structure and commissions are the dominant remuneration system, these financial planning businesses cannot simply 'turn off' the system within which they have to operate, so many elect to rebate all up-front and trailing commissions back to their clients. Although these qualities do not necessarily ensure clients receive good advice, it is a good starting point, and it's something that a wise client would insist on.

There are organisations within the industry that promote the services of these businesses. Independence in a financial planning sense should have a specific definition, but at this stage it does not. In our view, to be able to call themselves independent, a financial planner should:

- rebate any commissions received from financial products back to clients
- not be owned by a financial institution.

A business simply calling itself 'independent' does not ensure independence according to our conditions. As an example of how tricky terminology is used to deceive consumers, of the Association of Independently Owned Financial Planners' 120 member firms, nine were caught in the Westpoint collapse. The fact that these 'independently owned' financial planning firms (or rather their clients) were caught in this collapse means that they might have been 'independent' from the big dealer groups, but they did not have enough integrity to turn their backs on the fat commissions from some financial products.

With a case strengthened by the industry reforms, high-profile surveillance campaigns by ASIC and the backlash against Westpoint, fee-for-service financial planners are becoming a growing force in Australian financial planning.

The first ASIC survey, conducted in 2003 with the Australian Consumers' Association, found the industry to be 'structurally corrupt'. It was the third such survey conducted in eight years by the ACA. Of the 124 financial plans issued to the 60 shadow shoppers participating in the survey, only two were regarded by a panel of experts as 'very good'. A whopping 29 per cent were regarded as OK and 51 per cent were regarded as borderline, poor or very poor.

The areas in which financial planners fell down included inappropriate advice, advice that did not address the client's needs and legal non-compliance.

The then chief executive officer of the ACA, Louise Sylvan, said at the time: 'At the base of many of these problems is the structure of the industry. Consumers tend to believe that financial planners are independent advice givers, assessing the marketplace for appropriate products, which will meet the consumers' objectives. Nothing could be further from the truth.'

The results of this survey received unprecedented media attention, given the results came out just as the financial services industry was coming to grips with the new *FSRA* regime. It also put the industry on high alert about what might happen following the introduction of choice of superannuation fund legislation in July 2005, enabling many Australians to select which superannuation vehicle to invest in.

And these fears were quickly realised. A surveillance campaign conducted by ASIC on superannuation switching in 2006 found that *16 per cent of the advice was not reasonable*, given the client's needs — that is, you have a one in six chance of getting bad advice. Other findings included:

- When clients were advised to switch funds, a third of the time it was without credible reasons and had the potential to leave the client worse off.
- Unreasonable advice was three to six times more common when the adviser had an actual conflict of interest over remuneration or product recommendations.
- Consumers found it difficult to detect bad advice.

- In 46 per cent of cases, advisers failed to issue a Statement of Advice, a mandatory written statement of the advice given and the reasons why.

These surveys coincide with ASIC's ban of inappropriate behaviour and the increased action taken by the Financial Industry Complaints Service on behalf of consumers.

Case study

Chris Morgan was left with permanent disabilities after a workplace accident.

Knowing he would never be able to join the workforce again, it was important to him that the money he received in a Workcover compensation payout be invested wisely.

Chris Morgan was 47 years old when he was badly injured at work.

He received a $195,000 Workcover payout and saw a financial planner recommended by his bank for investment advice.

The father of three children, aged 9, 14, and 16, admits to 'not knowing anything about financial investments', and he relied heavily on the expertise of the adviser.

It was agreed that an allocated pension fund be created to generate an after-tax income of $400 a week to cover normal living expenses, over a potential investment period of 35 years. The model was based on an annual growth of his capital of 8 per cent.

'I was told my money was safe and that it would grow,' Chris Morgan says.

However less than a year later the payments were reduced to $351 a week as a result of a capital reduction due to a downturn in the market.

Mr Morgan subsequently closed the investment on the basis that if his funds continued to fall at the same rate for the next few years 'there would be nothing left'.

'To me it was snowballing and it didn't look like I would have any money left, so I decided to close it. Overall I lost $48,000 of my original investment.'

The Financial Industry Complaints Service assessed Mr Morgan's claim, which actually amounted to a loss of $16,851, after taking into account the $30,281 allocated pension payments that had been made during the term of the investment.

The planner stood by his advice, saying the investment was suitable and that he had explained how the concept of an allocated pension worked, including volatility principles. But the ruling panel disagreed:

'The most basic analysis by the member (financial adviser) showed that even an allocated pension at maximum drawdown was never going to meet the complainant's (Mr Morgan's) income needs – a projection at 8 per cent even before fees would produce a shortfall.'

The financial adviser was ordered to pay $16,851 plus interest to Mr Morgan, together with 50 per cent of the fees he had charged.

The panel was NOT asked to rule on Mr Morgan's irate reaction to news of his under-performing investment – namely, using sheep-dip to paint unflattering remarks about the financial adviser on his car.

Chapter 3

WHO ARE THE FINANCIAL PLANNERS?

Becoming a financial planner

In discussions about the financial planning industry's slow evolution, comment must be made about the education standards of the industry. Those standards are still low — it is possible to do an eight-day, exam-free course and become a financial planner — although there are definite moves to lift the educational standards. These include moves to increase the standards for the Certified Financial Planner (CFP) designation to include a completed undergraduate degree from 2007.

Anyone who wants to set up shop as a 'Financial Planner' must meet two standards.

First they must complete a course of study, as prescribed by the Australian Securities & Investments Commission (ASIC). These educational requirements are discussed later in the chapter, although it is reasonable to say they are not very onerous, particularly when compared to professions such as medicine, accountancy, law or even primary school teaching. Compared to most professions, financial planning is a breeze to qualify for.

Second, the agent must be licensed to provide personal financial advice. This licensing comes in one of two forms.

The first is with a financial services licence, issued by ASIC. It is time-consuming and expensive to maintain a financial services licence and, as the statistics in the previous chapter show, this is the less common option.

Rather than get their own financial services licence, most financial planners choose to become an 'authorised representative' of a larger dealer group. This 'authorised representative' status allows them to provide personal financial advice, and, as with any franchise, the planner pays a fee to the dealer group to be an authorised representative. In return they receive technical assistance, training, help with compliance and, usually, an approved investment list to recommend to clients.

The 'normal' career progression for a financial planner goes along the lines of:

1 Start working in a financial planning firm in a 'client services' role. This is primarily an administrative role, which includes placing investments and helping keep track of client portfolios.
2 Move to a 'paraplanning' role. Paraplanning is increasingly considered a career in itself, and involves much of the technical 'behind the scenes' financial planning work, such as preparing Statements of Advice (financial plans) and portfolio reviews.
3 Take on a role as a fully-fledged financial planner.

Of course there are many paths into financial planning. Another common one is to move into it from accountancy.

Educational requirements for financial planners

The minimum educational standards to be a financial planner are not high. The shortest educational program is called PS146, which offers an eight-day, exam-free course that allows people to earn a 'Diploma of Financial Services' and meet the educational requirements for becoming a financial planner. A further eight-day course is available for those financial planners who want to upgrade their qualifications to an 'Advanced Diploma of Financial Services'.

The 'Diploma of Financial Services' is the basic qualification for financial planners. This is usually a course comprising four subjects, with the expectation of about 40 to 60 hours work required to complete each subject. The 'Advanced Diploma of Financial Services' is an upgrade qualification that requires a further four subjects.

The educational requirements for a financial planner are set out in the ASIC policy statement PS146. The requirements boil down to a 'training register', which lists the subjects and courses that can be completed by a financial planner to meet the educational standards to provide advice on different areas of financial planning. This is where the familiar term 'PS146 compliant' originates from; it refers to a financial planner who has met the educational requirements on the ASIC training register. The Diploma of Financial Services and Advanced Diploma of Financial Services degrees are designed to meet these educational standards, and thus to be listed on the ASIC training register.

The Certified Financial Planner designation, CFP, is another commonly seen financial planning qualification. In Australia, the CFP designation is awarded by the Financial Planning Association (FPA). The FPA describes the CFP qualification as the 'the highest professional certification that can be awarded to a financial planner'.

From 1 January 2007 to be awarded CFP status a financial planner must meet the following standards. They must have:

- an approved undergraduate or postgraduate qualification (this is a new requirement)

- an education consisting of either four CFP subjects, or an exemption based on the completion of an approved course
- completed a 'certification assessment'
- had three years of approved practitioner experience
- agreed to abide by the FPA Code of Ethics and Rules of Professional Conduct.

It is worth noting that the requirements to be awarded a CFP have been strengthened since the designation was first issued, so not all current CFP holders have actually met this standard. There is also an increasing range of courses providing education for financial planners above the minimum standards. For example, several universities are now offering undergraduate or postgraduate courses in financial planning.

The trend towards improvement in the educational standards of financial planners is positive, but right now caution needs to be taken to really understand the academic qualifications of any financial planner you are considering working with — you don't want to find out that your trusted adviser has no more than a couple of weeks of training.

Licensing and the dealer group structure

As well as meeting educational requirements, a financial planner must either hold an Australian Financial Services Licence (AFSL), or be an 'authorised representative' of a licence holder. The financial and administrative costs associated with holding an AFSL provide a deterrent to individual financial planners. That means that the majority of financial planners work as employees of financial planning businesses, or set up their own businesses as 'authorised representatives' of dealer groups.

The financial planner pays a fee to the dealer group for this service. Generally the fee is a percentage of the revenue generated by the planner, often 10–25 per cent. There are also dealer groups that charge a flat fee, often in the range of $1–3000 a month. In return for this fee, the dealer group will provide the planner with a number of inputs that they need to operate a financial planning firm. These may include:

- support to meet the compliance standards set for financial planners
- access to financial planning software
- templates for important documents, such as Statements of Advice (financial plans) and financial services guides
- marketing and business development support
- ongoing professional development opportunities
- client referrals
- technical assistance
- an approved product list for the financial planner to operate from
- model portfolios and asset allocation guidelines.

The financial planner has to make it clear which dealer group that they are authorised through, so you should see this on business cards, Financial Services Guides and the Statements of Advice.

Westpoint

Recently another weakness has shown up in the structure of the financial planning industry, particularly in the licensing arrangements. Alison Maynard, chief executive of the Financial Industry Complaints Service (FICS), said, 'There are numerous examples in Westpoint cases where a member [of FICS, which includes all licensees] put the business into administration and has gone into business as an authorised representative of another member.' She also said, 'We're talking about ordinary people with life savings or retirement funds being advised by a licence holder who can cease to trade when there's a problem, and then go into business as an authorised representative for someone else, or open up under a new licence. That is a serious issue.'

It is distressing to see this happen with financial planners who have failed their clients in the most serious manner. They simply set up a new practice under a new licence or as an authorised representative of another licensee.

It may seem somewhat unfair to criticise financial planners for the collapse of an investment, particularly as serious questions have been raised about the role of the auditor and the integrity of Westpoint boss Norm Carey. However, we have spoken to a number of Westpoint victims and we can confirm that some financial planners involved in selling Westpoint investments were guilty of many misdeeds, such as:

- *Regularly suggesting that somehow Westpoint had found a way of getting high investment returns (around 12 per cent) with low risk.* This contravenes the first lesson of 'Investment Theory 101', where risk and reward must be related. Ignoring this investment fundamental is either ignorance or incompetence.
- *Not understanding the investment.* Don't blame the auditor — Westpoint was a high-risk mezzanine debt investment in property construction. Recommending the investment as low risk was either dishonesty or incompetence. Reports that financial planners recommended it to clients as being 'like investing in a bank' are horrifying.
- *Ignoring asset allocation and diversification.* The number-one tool that investors have at their disposal to manage investment risk is diversification and asset allocation. Yet many investors advised by financial planners put the majority of their assets into the one investment company (Westpoint) in one relatively obscure asset class (mezzanine finance). One of the professional cornerstones of a financial planner must be the

ability to build effective investment portfolios, using asset allocation and diversification to manage risk. Financial planners who recommended the majority of any client's portfolio be held in Westpoint grossly failed this test of professional standards.

- *Encouraging investors to borrow against their home to invest in Westpoint, when they had specified that they were looking for a 'low-risk' investment strategy.* Westpoint, like any mezzanine finance investment, was risky. Borrowing money to invest increases the risk profile of any investment. For clients looking for a low-risk investment strategy, borrowing to invest in mezzanine finance is not appropriate. Look at the consequences: investors struggling to keep their family home after they mortgaged it to invest in Westpoint.

A group of financial planners caused immense damage to clients through conduct that ranged from incompetence to dishonesty, and which was professionally inept by any standard. So what happens to them under the current financial planning industry structure? They continue to practise as financial planners.

The role of research

An important part of being an informed financial planning consumer is to understand the role of research and 'the approved product' list. The approved product list is a summary of all the investments and products that financial planners operating at a firm can recommend to clients. It will include such things as:

- managed funds
- wraps/platforms
- insurance providers
- direct shares.

From a consumer's perspective, the important thing to note is that the approved product list represents the 'universe' of investments available for that particular financial planner to recommend. It's put together by the research arm of the financial planning firm, and there is pressure on a financial planning firm to approve products associated with the holder of the licence for the firm. Is this because they are the best funds available for consumers, or because they are (for example) AMP products?

An example of the conflict between compiling approved product lists, and whether these lists are in the best interest of consumers, is industry superannuation funds. In Australia industry super funds represent some of the lowest-cost, and best-performing investment options available. Yet they end up on very few dealer group approved product lists.

For about two years AMP had these funds on its approved product list. Towards the middle of 2006 industry funds were removed from the list, so AMP financial planners were no longer able to recommend them. Suddenly industry super funds, which are generally the best-performing, lowest-cost investment options available, were no longer available to AMP clients.

Approved product lists are not all bad. They provide a level of restraint on individual financial planners who may be inclined towards making outlandish recommendations. For example, there has been no suggestion that any financial planner associated with the biggest financial institutions, such as AMP, the big four banks or AXA, were caught recommending Westpoint to their investors. It is unlikely that such an investment would ever make it onto their approved list. That said, it is important that investors bear in mind the restrictive role that an approved product list plays in directing a financial planner's recommendations.

The company behind the brand

A challenge for consumers is understanding the network of relationships between financial planning businesses, their owners and related financial products. It is not difficult to understand that when you walk into an AMP financial planning firm, you are likely to receive advice that favours AMP products. It's more difficult, however, for consumers walking into a Hillross Financial Planning office, an Arrive Wealth Management office, or a Magnify Financial Planners office — all of which are owned by AMP — to know who the advice will be favouring.

These less-obvious ownership relationships are disclosed, but often not prominently. The problem of not being sure which financial planning 'brand' is owned by which financial services company is also a factor with large financial institutions, fund managers and financial product providers. For example, National Australia Bank owns MLC, Commonwealth Bank owns Colonial, ING is 49 per cent owned by ANZ, St George Bank owns Asgard and Advance Funds Management, and Westpac owns BT.

In an industry where conflicts of interest have to be at the forefront of consumers' minds, this difficult network of ownership is another challenge to be unravelled. The following table outlines a number of financial planning firms, and ownership interest in these firms by large financial services institutions.

Advisory firm	Ownership interest
Ipac	AXA
Monitor Money	AXA
AMP Financial Planning	AMP
Hillross Financial Services	AMP
Arrive Wealth Management	AMP
Colonial Financial Planning	Commonwealth Bank

Advisory firm	*Ownership interest*
Financial Wisdom	Commonwealth Bank
MLC Financial Planning	National Australia Bank
Garvan Financial Planning	National Australia Bank
Securitor	St George Bank
PACT	St George Bank
RetireInvest	ING

The AMP advantage

We have talked a lot about financial planners from a consumer perspective and some aspects of the industry to be wary of. It is also worth considering how the large financial services institutions, which have the largest force of financial planners, view the importance of planners to their business.

Of the major financial services companies, AMP has the largest number of financial planners in Australia; as of June 2006, it had 1553 planners. National Australia Bank had the next largest force, with 1311 and ANZ/ING had 1106.

It is therefore interesting to look at how AMP communicates the role of financial planners to AMP shareholders, and see how financial planners fit within the AMP business model. In a presentation to JP Morgan conferences, listed as an ASX announcement in September 2006, AMP identified six drivers of its business. One was distribution, a reference to the role that financial planners play in getting other drivers, including products, platforms and asset management, to consumers. Indeed, in the same presentation, AMP focused on its 'comparative advantage' in 'planner distribution'. This boils down to a boast that compared with the competition it had more and better financial planners distributing their products.

In talking about the financial planning 'value chain', which refers to all the activities involved for a client in a financial-planning relationship, AMP noted that its business model allows it to 'capture' the profits across the entire value chain. This is done with an AMP financial planner recommending an AMP-related portfolio administration platform with AMP asset management. In this model, AMP estimates that the pricing it captures is:

- 0.75–1.15 per cent on dealer group/financial planning service
- 0.4–0.95 per cent on platforms (portfolio administration)
- 0.2–0.4 per cent on asset management.

How effective is this for AMP? Their 2006 half-year annual-results presentation noted that of every dollar invested for clients by AMP Financial Services, 60 cents flowed into AMP Future Directions Funds, a range of multi-manager funds managed by AMP Capital Investors and Mercers Investment Consulting, and 21 cents flowed directly to AMP Capital Investor's Funds. Therefore, 81 cents in every dollar overseen by AMP financial services ends up in AMP platforms.

How financial planners generate income

There are four basic fee models that describe way the majority of financial planning practices earn income from clients. These are:

1 fee-for-service financial planning practices, which charge an hourly rate and accept no other fees (such as commissions)
2 fee-for-service financial planning practices that charge a percentage fee based on the size of a client's portfolio
3 commission-based financial planners who have their income paid to them through the financial products that they

recommend to clients, such as managed funds, wraps and insurances

4 financial planners who charge both a fee and take a commission, usually ongoing trailing commissions.

The first two models are similar, and the most 'independent' — the financial planners charge a fee and either recommend investment solutions that don't pay any commission, or rebate any commissions received to the client.

The difference between these fee models lies in two points. First, percentage-based fees sometimes makes it difficult for a client to fully grasp the magnitude of the fees they are paying. For example, a fee structure that charges an annual fee of 1 per cent of the portfolio value up to $500,000 and 0.5 per cent of the portfolio value beyond that results in a client with a $1 million portfolio paying a $10,000 annual fee. Second, the hourly rate-based fee means the compensation the financial planner receives is tied to the level of service they provide. This fee model is similar to the billing process of other professions, such as accountants and lawyers.

The third model (the commission model) dominates the industry. It is the cornerstone of the conflict of interest issues that surround the industry and, thus, is dealt with in detail in this book.

The fourth model, where both a fee and a commission are taken, can also be confusing to clients. Because of the emphasis on 'fee-for-service' as the preferred financial planning model for many consumers, they don't realise that in addition to paying a fee, they are also paying trailing commissions out of their investments. Every client of a financial planning firm should understand whether they are paying any trailing commissions, and should not underestimate the long-term effect that paying an ongoing trailing fee has on the value of their overall portfolio.

Case study

Ben Mackenzie thought investing in a grape vineyard was a smart way to earn money and minimise tax. But the scheme was affected by the drought and it failed to bear fruit.

Ben Mackenzie had invested in three tax-effective schemes over three years and after receiving advice from his accountant who was also his financial planner, he decided to invest in another similar agribusiness project.

The scheme was a vineyard investment, which involved investors or 'growers' making an up-front payment and an additional payment the following year.

By the third year, according to projections, the vineyard's operating costs would be recovered through the sale of grapes and bottled or bulk wine.

However, prospectus forecasts were not met, largely as a result of the drought, but also because mass vine plantings created a wine glut and prices dropped.

In accordance with the licence deed, the project manager requested additional funds from the growers to maintain the vineyard's viability.

Mr Mackenzie had invested a total of $55,900 in the project and decided against injecting further capital.

As a result, he lost his entire investment when the scheme collapsed. Those investors who did make additional payments converted their entitlement into shares when the scheme became an unlisted public company.

Mr Mackenzie claims he was not made aware of the structure and nature of the investment or the risks involved. He says that despite the fact the project was a tax-effective scheme, it was sold to him as an investment.

He claims that he expected to receive a return after three years and had no idea there was a chance he would be asked to make additional payments in the long term.

Mr Mackenzie took his concerns to the Financial Industry Complaints Service seeking compensation for the money he lost. The ruling panel found the financial adviser had not breached his duty of care because his client understood the nature of the investment and the risks involved.

But it ruled there was a shortfall in the financial adviser's performance because he should have kept Mr Mackenzie informed of the vineyard's financial decline. It ruled:

'He had no expectation that he might have to prop up the investment long term and when he continued to receive bills he was not offered any advice or assistance on what his options were.'

As a result, the panel ordered the financial planner to refund the commission he received on the vineyard investment, plus interest.

Chapter 4

YOUR RESPONSIBILITIES

Getting advice

If ever an industry is suited to the consumer warning 'let the buyer beware', it would be the financial services industry. With it's complex structure of commissions, ownership, distribution and advice, it is hard for any consumer to understand and navigate. And yet, with the onus increasingly on each of us to be financially independent, it is very important to find a financial planner with the skills to understand financial goals, set a plan to meet those goals and monitor and motivate until those goals are met.

The answer for many is not to completely give up on the industry — although the option of 'doing it yourself' is discussed later in the book — you should think about how you can most effectively approach and manage a successful financial planning relationship.

The first, and perhaps most important, step in approaching advice is to be educated about the financial services industry so you are an informed consumer. This is crucial in an industry with such complex relationships and payments for financial services.

Having built an understanding of the financial services industry, a positive second step is to set up a reasonable outline of the sort of financial planner you would like to work with. At the end of Chapter 11 are some of the questions ASIC suggests be put to prospective financial planner. These would be a good starting point for putting together a model of which characteristics you would like in a financial planner — from experience and qualifications to the way they charge fees.

A good third step to approaching advice, then, is to start searching for a financial planner with the characteristics you have identified. Sources of information include family and friends, other professionals, such as accountants and solicitors, the internet and professional financial planning bodies.

Then you need to weigh the alternatives and decide who to proceed with. Later in this chapter we look at what to expect from the financial planning process. There is usually an introductory meeting and initial communication where you can further assess whether the financial planner you have chosen is the right one for you. If not, you should be comfortable ending the relationship there.

This overall process is consistent with the common basic model of consumer decision-making:

1 Recognising the need (deciding that you want to work with a financial planner).
2 Search of information on services that could satisfy the needs of the buyer (identifying what you are looking for in a financial planner).
3 Alternative selection (weighing up the alternatives).
4 Decision-making (making the choice to proceed).
5 Post-purchase behaviour (assessing whether your expectations were met).

However, the consumer's role in the financial planning process does not end when they find the right planner; that's just the beginning.

Preparing for financial planning

The process of seeking financial advice means that the individual is looking for *personal financial advice*, rather than *general financial advice*. Each of these is defined in law. Personal advice means advice that is tailored to an individual's needs, situation, and financial goals. The onus is on the consumer to provide correct information to the financial planners, so they can prepare appropriately tailored advice.

In most cases the financial planner will provide the client with some sort of questionnaire to complete. The questionnaire will gather information on several important areas. These include:

- Personal details — basic details such as your age, family situation, employment details, contact details and so on.
- Your current financial position: your assets and liabilities. This is the starting position the financial planner will work from.
- Information about your financial goals, for example, when you would like to retire and what level of retirement income you would like. This should be the core of what the financial planner is working towards: meeting your financial goals or working with you to modify them to more realistic levels.
- Information about your cash flow — details such as how much you earn, how much you spend and what surplus is left for investment purposes. The key here is surplus income; that is, what income the financial planner has to work with to establish strategies that will improve your financial position and allow you to meet your financial goals.
- Information about the 'contingency planning' you have in place. This is in case something goes wrong. It will include

looking at existing levels of life insurance and your estate planning arrangements. Part of the planning process is to consider what would happen financially if you were killed or badly injured; to organise your financial situation to help you and your family cope as well as possible with these situations.

- Information about your 'risk tolerance' or 'risk profile'. Your risk tolerance is your level of comfort with investment volatility, as well as issues about your investment strategy, such as investment time frame and investment experience. The financial planner will then make any investment recommendations with your risk tolerance in mind.

The client questionnaire is a key document in the financial planning process because it provides the information the planner works from to build the plan for your situation. Often financial planners may require more detailed information from you so they can look further into your situation.

At this point, a planner may ask you to sign a letter giving them authority to access details of an investment or superannuation account. For example, they may want to find out more about the life insurance cover that you have in your superannuation fund, or the investment strategy for your superannuation account. They will ask you to sign a letter that states you have given them, as a financial planner, authority to discuss your superannuation account with your superannuation provider.

Documentation

During the financial planning process you should be careful to *keep and file* the important paperwork that you receive. The key documents (and their almost inevitable three-letter acronyms) are listed here.

Financial Services Guide (FSG)

You must receive this document as part of the financial planning process. It gives you information about who is giving you advice, their background, what areas they can advise on, how they will be paid for the advice, how they are licensed to provide advice, and how you can lodge a complaint if you need to. (There is more about the complaints process later in this chapter.)

Statement of Advice (SOA)

The Statement of Advice is the main document your financial planner prepares for you. It is what would previously have been referred to as the financial plan.

Section 947B of the *Corporations Act 2001* summarises the key components that are required in a Statement of Advice. These key components include:

- the statement setting out the advice — what the financial planner is advising you to do
- the basis of the advice — why it is suitable given your needs; that is, how the advice will help you to meet your financial goals
- contact details about the financial planner (as the Authorised Representative) and the licensee who is providing this advice to you. It is important that this relationship and the details for both are clear to you.
- information about how the financial planner is getting paid and all other fees associated with the Statement of Advice (such as managed fund fees, wrap fees and insurance premiums)
- details about any relationship that might influence the financial planner's advice (for example, holding shares in the company of a fund manager they are recommending)
- any relationship the financial planner or the financial service licence holder might have that could influence the advice

(for example, the firm the financial planner works for might be owned by AMP, which may influence them to recommend AMP investments).

Statement of Additional Advice (SOAA) or Record of Advice (ROA)

These are supplementary documents a financial planner may give to provide further advice after previously issuing a SOA. They will be briefer versions of an SOA, although no less important, and will include further personal financial advice.

Product Disclosure Statement (PDS)

The Product Disclosure Statement provides the details of the financial product that is being recommended to you. ASIC Policy Statement (PS) 168 emphasises that a Product Disclosure Statement must be provided to you before you act on any financial planning recommendations. This document includes details about the risks, benefits and costs of the financial product that has been recommended to you.

Range of advice

When you receive personal financial advice from a planner, it may be either in the form of comprehensive financial advice, which entails a full review of your situation, or limited financial advice, which means that the advice only deals with a specific aspect of your situation.

Comprehensive financial advice

Let's consider what should be involved in a comprehensive review of a person's situation. The key components of your personal situation, reviewed within the framework of comprehensive financial advice, should include:

- a review to ensure that your estate planning (wills and power of attorney arrangements) is adequate
- checking that your life insurance situation is sound

- possibly commenting on your general insurance/health insurance situation
- recommendations for your financial planning strategy and the 'basis of advice' — that is, how these recommendations will help you meet your financial goals. Financial planning strategy means the ongoing plan you have to meet your financial goals. Examples of common strategies include salary sacrificing to superannuation, making additional mortgage repayments or using an allocated pension to fund your retirement.
- recommendations for any investments or other financial product, such as wraps or insurance
- a summary of your personal details and situation, including income and expenses and your financial situation, on which the advice is based.

This comprehensive financial advice will be set out in a Statement of Advice, as discussed earlier in this chapter, which will also set out all the costs associated with the recommendations and the financial planning service.

Limited financial advice

It may be that you are seeking financial advice about only a portion of your financial situation, which is where limited financial advice may be provided. A common example of this would be someone who has changed jobs and wants advice on investing their superannuation; just this one part of their financial affairs. In this case the person would stipulate that this is all they are looking for advice on, and the financial planner would prepare and implement a 'Limited Statement of Advice'. This will still address the same issues of fees, who the financial planner is licensed through and relationships that might influence their advice, and it will include a statement that outlines the limited scope of the advice.

What to expect

It is difficult to draft what a 'normal' outline financial planning process looks like because it will vary significantly from firm to firm. The following is a chronological look at what might constitute a reasonably typical financial planning experience.

Step 1: Contact the financial planning firm and ask for an initial appointment

It is often at this point that you will be sent the Financial Services Guide, which outlines information about the financial planner. Many firms also send out the client questionnaire at this stage for you to complete and return. Some, however, wait until after the first appointment to do this.

Step 2: The first appointment

This is still part of the fact-finding stage of the financial planning relationship. It is a chance for the client to meet the financial planner and see how comfortable they feel with them. It gives the financial planner a chance to gather further information about the client's situation, discuss it in general terms and offer thoughts about how they might progress. At this stage, you should be able to ask any questions you have and ensure that you are comfortable working with the financial planner.

Firms that have paraplanners may have them sit in on this initial meeting. Paraplanners work with financial planners and offer them technical support. Often it is the paraplanner who prepares the Statement of Advice, in consultation with the financial planner, so it is useful for them to meet you, and be part of this meeting.

Step 3: Statement of Advice

After the initial meeting there is usually some trigger that allows you to let the financial planner know that you want to proceed with the financial planning relationship. For example, you might be asked to sign a letter of engagement. After you have done this the financial planner will go about preparing the Statement of Advice and the paperwork that helps with the implementation of advice, for example, Product Disclosure Statements and application forms.

It can take some time for a Statement of Advice to be written. It is worth establishing a time frame before this process starts so that you know what to expect.

Step 4: Statement of Advice presentation meeting

Once the Statement of Advice is prepared, it will be sent to you, along with the other paperwork needed to implement the financial plan. This is done in a variety of ways. Some firms mail the paperwork to the client and ask them to return it; others have a meeting in which to present the Statement of Advice and to start the paperwork.

Step 5: Implementation

A key part of the financial planning process is the implementation of the recommendations. In large financial planning firms a third tier of staff, often known as client service managers, will put together all the paperwork, establish investments and keep you updated on the progress of your situation.

Step 6: Expectations of an ongoing relationship

Once the dust has settled, and the initial recommendations are implemented, it is important to understand what ongoing financial planning support is provided. This may range from six-monthly reviews if you have a large portfolio, through to having to pay for any extra reviews, if and when you need them. It is important to understand up-front the level of ongoing service and to ensure you are comfortable with it and that it is consistent with the ongoing fees and/or commissions you are paying.

It is worth repeating what was said at the start of this section: that every planner will have a slightly different way of providing financial planning advice. At some level or another, these six steps will play a role in the way most financial planners structure their client relationships, with the main steps in the process being information gathering, preparation of the Statement of Advice and implementation of the plan.

How to complain

ASIC, the regulator of the financial services industry, produced a policy statement (PS139) that deals specifically with the setting up of complaints resolution schemes for the financial services industry. This is done as part of its role in monitoring the financial services industry and in promoting consumer protection.

All Australian Financial Services Licence holders that offer advice to retail investors, as a condition of their licence, have to be part of an external complaints resolution scheme. To this end, the Financial Industry Complaints Service (FICS) was established as the external complaints resolution scheme of choice in the financial services industry. FICS is a scheme that hears complaints by consumers against the financial services licensees who nominate FICS as their external complaints resolution scheme.

However, before any complaint is made by a client to an external complaints resolution scheme, it is likely that efforts will have to be made to resolve the complaint internally. Of course, this is potentially the cheapest and quickest way to resolve the problem for both the client and the financial planner, so it makes sense to start there.

Both the internal complaints process and the process to access the external complaints resolution scheme (FICS) will be set out in the Financial Services Guide, the document your financial planner must give you early on in the financial planning process. (If you lose it at any stage, just ask for another copy.)

There are usually three stages of complaint resolution outlined. The first is to approach the financial planner directly and try to resolve the situation with them. If this is not done satisfactorily within a set time frame (often one or two weeks), the next step is usually to lodge a written complaint with the financial services licence holder you are dealing with. There will be a specified time frame in which they must respond to the compliant, usually four to six weeks. If you are still not happy at this stage, the next step is to lodge a complaint with FICS. The contact details for FICS are:

Toll-free Phone:	1300 780 808
Address:	PO Box 579
	Collins St West
	Melbourne Vic 8007
Web:	www.fics.asn.au

The website includes FICS determinations and adjudications, which give you some idea about how their decisions are reached.

ASIC also has a free-call infoline on 1300 300 630, which you may use to make a complaint and obtain information about your rights.

Given the role that FICS plays in escalating your complaint beyond the financial planner and financial service licence holder you are dealing with, it is worth knowing a little more about this scheme. The members of FICS are the financial service licence holders who nominate FICS as their external disputes resolutions scheme, and it is these members who fund FICS. Because of this, FICS is a free service for consumers who have complaints concerning the financial services industry. FICS, in its own literature, reports that only a small proportion of cases take more than 12 months to resolve; that is, most cases are resolved within 12 months. The dollar-value limit on claims is:

- $250,000 for life insurance
- $6000 per month for income protection insurance
- $100,000 for other financial services.

FICS seeks to resolve cases by first contacting the financial services provider involved and then, if no resolution comes about, through referring the case to the FICS panel for a written decision.

If you find yourself in a situation where you feel that you have a significant complaint or problem with any part of the financial planning process that can't immediately be solved directly with the planner involved, then it makes sense to seek legal advice. The process of internal complaints resolution with the financial planning firm you are dealing with, and then the FICS process, will take time. If the situation is significant, seeking legal advice at the start of this process makes sense. You should not feel compelled to simply fit within the industry scheme guidelines, and consulting a lawyer provides you with someone who can discuss your situation, suggest ways of proceeding and assist during the process.

The aftermath of the Westpoint collapse is providing the complaints resolution system with its biggest test. The previous chapter identified one problem with the current licensing scheme shown up by Westpoint, with financial planners who had recommended Westpoint changing their financial services licence and continuing to practice. Another problem is appearing with many Westpoint victims having claims for amounts ranging from $100–500,000, which puts them above the FICS range of $100,000, but without a large enough claim to justify the significant costs associated with litigation through the court system. No doubt, as the Westpoint case evolves, more will be learnt about the effectiveness of the financial services complaints system.

Conclusion

Given that a good financial planner can be an ally in creating wealth over time, it is important to think about how, as a client, you can best manage the process of accessing financial planning advice. Getting good financial planning advice is not all about the adviser, and will take some effort on your behalf, especially in terms of providing initial information to the financial planner, and in the implementation stage. Seeking financial advice can mean either having someone comprehensively review your financial situation, or simply receiving advice on one area of your situation. Of course, not everything goes well all the time, and being armed with advice on the complaints options available to you is important if things do happen to go wrong.

Case study

Rose Chan was faced with having to decide what to do with the proceeds of her son's estate. She invested in a shares fund on the advice of a financial planner, without understanding the risks.

Rose Chan first met her financial adviser at her bank, where money left by her late son had been sitting in a balanced fund and a share income fund, earning a modest return.

They developed an investment strategy aimed at providing a modest income to support her simple lifestyle and supplement her pension.

Ms Chan said she wanted to safeguard her late son's estate and that security of the investment was more important to her than wealth creation.

After the meeting, the financial adviser drew up an executive summary, which stated:

'Our recommendations will enable you to achieve the following:

- Minimise your tax liabilities.
- Ensure your capital does not diminish early in retirement and your income increases with inflation.
- Enjoy your lifestyle without being concerned with your financial affairs.
- Be organised and in control of your financial affairs.
- Structure your cash flow so it is received on a regular basis.'

It went on to say that a minimum return of 6 per cent was achievable and that little or no tax would be paid each year.

Over 12 months, Ms Chan put $410,000 into a shares fund, including $200,000 from the sale of a property.

The product had a 29 per cent weighting to international shares, 43 per cent Australian shares, 6 per cent Australian property securities, 2 per cent international property and infrastructure and 5 per cent to private equity.

It was intended the investment would be for a minimum of 5 years however less than half way into the timeline Ms Chan opted out, crystallising a loss of $102,135.

She claims the details of the fund were never explained and she never understood what she was buying.

'The potential volatility of the investment was never explained to me. The adviser never attempted to make me aware of the risk of having a total of 85 per cent exposure to equity and property markets.I believe this constitutes a gross lack of duty of care.'

Ms Chan's financial adviser denied any liability, stating that she had accepted and signed three separate financial needs analysis documents.

The Financial Industry Complaints Service panel ruled that the adviser's executive summary effectively conveyed Ms Chan a guarantee of performance to the extent that her investments were guaranteed to increase in value at a minimum of 6 per cent above inflation.

'The recommendations in the executive summary are so positive that the complainant or a reasonable person in her position would not find it necessary to go through the whole of the plan or place much weight on the disclaimers if they did.'

The panel ruled the financial adviser should pay $30,000 plus interest.

The compensation amount was based on the outcome of her money being invested using a more conservative strategy.

Chapter 5

THE LIMITS AND PITFALLS OF ADVICE

Getting the right adviser

Actually the real problem is finding someone you like and trust, who is going to give you unbiased, independent advice. You've probably got this message by now, but we think the fundamental problem with the financial advice industry in this country is that the line between advice and sales has blurred: you never really know when someone is telling you what you need to know, what's in your best interests, or just giving you a sales pitch.

There is also the problem of finding someone with the right qualifications — or any qualifications at all. Knowing which financial professionals can provide what advice is just the first step to not only getting the right advice, but also protecting yourself against a sales pitch masquerading as advice.

The second (and possibly more important) step, is tempering your own expectations of what's possible. A factor in bad financial advice is many people's ignorance about some of the basic principles of investing, in particular the principle of risk and reward.

The most common form of inappropriate advice from a financial adviser is that a particular investment will provide a fantastic return in complete safety. It won't. But unfortunately bad advice — and not just the high-risk sales pitch — is alive and well in the financial services industry, despite increased licensing and training requirements for all financial services professionals.

And it seems the professions involved in the provision of information and advice (financial planners, insurance agents, accountants and stockbrokers) have all had their fair share of scandals. It seems that every week newspapers report on investors who have been on the wrong end of dud advice, given by unqualified people launching illegal investment schemes promising the earth. Too often investors are lured by the promise of high returns over a short time, otherwise known as a 'fast buck', and they get sucked in by a smooth sales pitch and big numbers.

But it's always the investor who suffers most (often their lives are ruined). Meanwhile, the maximum penalty for the unscrupulous provider of such advice is a mere $22,000 fine, five years' jail or both.

Westpoint is one of the more high-profile investment scandals you may have read about.

It seems that no level of industry regulation can stamp out lies and deception entirely. In fact, outrageous financial schemes even have their own awards. The Australian Securities & Investments Commission's annual 'Pie in the Sky' awards are designed to warn investors to be 'buyer beware' and to remind them that unfortunately such schemes do exist.

Take the 2006 winner. Through wealth seminars, Craig McKim of the Pegasus Leveraged Options Group, promoted an illegal investment scheme that promised a weekly return of 8 per cent. That's right, a weekly return of 8 per cent — that's above what most asset classes return in a year! McKim managed to raise $3.7 million from 90 investors and promptly blew more than $2 million of it on gambling and private expenses. He is now in jail.

Clients' knowledge base is usually called 'financial literacy', which is as good a name as any for basic familiarity with what's going on. It doesn't mean having a degree in finance and being able to completely do it yourself; it means understanding some basic concepts about the financial services industry so you can develop a radar for when things appear too good to be true.

Over the past few years, the government has increasingly turned its attention to trying to increase the financial literacy of Australians, although (as with a lot of bureaucratic projects) you would have to say its effectiveness has been slow to get going. But at least it's having a go.

In February 2004 the federal government established the Consumer and Financial Literacy Taskforce to develop a first-ever national strategy. In its first discussion paper, titled 'Australian consumers and money: Helping people to manage their money better', the taskforce found there were more than 700 consumer information initiatives in the market, creating a high level of confusion among consumers.

The taskforce recognised that the complexity in the financial system was inhibiting many Australians from reaching our financial goals. 'Overspending, overborrowing, underinsuring, scams, schemes and the complexity of financial products and processes need to be avoided, understood or overcome to achieve financial success,' said taskforce chairman Paul Clitheroe.

It is a big problem to overcome, particularly when history has shown that even the most educated of us can still get lured into investments by the promise of double-digit returns. According to ASIC, in the past six years at least 6000 Australians have lost about $500 million of their life savings chasing high returns.

Couple this with results from the 2005 ANZ Financial Literacy Research, which found that 47 per cent of respondents would make some sort of investment after seeing advertising for an investment offering a return 'well above market rates at no extra risk', and you can see why so many people lose money.

So what is regarded as high returns? A good rule of thumb is if a scheme promises you 1.5–2 per cent or more per year better than the average return for that type of asset, approach with caution. If it's any higher than that, don't approach at all!

But probably the best advice is the simplest: if it sounds too good to be true, it probably is. If you get stung, working with a complaint resolution scheme is really your only option, and certainly the cheapest. Taking your own legal action is very expensive and class actions, such as the one that has been launched against the promoters of the Westpoint scheme, are rare.

Under the *Financial Services Reform Act 2001* (*FSRA*), all Australian Financial Services Licence (AFSL) holders that deal with retail clients must be a member of an approved external dispute resolution scheme.

The Financial Industry Complaints Service (FICS), is the main one, and provides free advice and assistance to investors. The process used by FICS is to first try and resolve complaints by mutual agreement between the parties. If this does not work, the matter is referred to the panel or the adjudicator, who has the ability to make a formal determination which is binding on the member. We'll talk more about how to complain shortly.

According to FICS statistics, in 2006 they received a total of 6543 telephone enquires and complaints. At the top of the list was life insurance, accounting for over 44 per cent of the complaints that progressed to investigation.

It was followed by financial planning (37.8 per cent), managed investments (8.9 per cent) and stockbroking (7.1 per cent). While these numbers are lower than in 2005, just one complaint is really one too many, especially if you are the one who has been left financially high and dry.

How to complain

According to ASIC, you have the right to complain if you are not happy with any aspect of a financial service or product. Your first port of call is to go back to the financial service provider or where you purchased the financial product and talk through the issues.

If you are still not satisfied, get a copy of their complaints procedure. This will probably state that you need to write a formal letter of complaint to the business. This is your next course of action.

If a letter does not bring the desired response, it is time to contact an independent complaints scheme. The financial institution's complaint procedure may include the name of the scheme of which they are a part, or you can just contact FICS or ASIC for further help.

The complaints scheme is free and acts independently of your interests or those of the financial institution. Remember that a complaints scheme will not help you unless you have already contacted the adviser or institution yourself to try and resolve the problem.

The complaints scheme will act as a mediator and if it cannot help you come to an agreed settlement, it will make the final decision. If you are not happy with the decision, your final course is legal action.

Note that to be eligible for access to the complaints resolution system that has been set under the financial services regulations, you must have dealt with a licensed financial adviser. The recent Westpoint debacle is a persuasive example. Some investors invested in this doomed property scheme by responding to newspaper advertisements or attending seminars, rather than by going through a licensed adviser. These people do not have access to an independent complaints scheme such as FICS.

Who can advise on what?

The simple answer to this question is that professionals can only advise on the areas in which they are licensed to do so.

There are two types of advice, personal and general. The difference is that an adviser providing personal advice takes into consideration your objectives and financial situation and then develops an appropriate strategy. General advice is more general information and does not take into account your objectives or financial situation.

The only people allowed to give personal advice are those professionals who either work for or who represent an advisory business that holds an Australian Financial Services Licence (AFSL).

There are currently approximately 4445 AFSL holders and more than 45,000 Authorised Representatives. In the Australian financial services industry, licensed advice covers superannuation, insurance, shares, managed funds and some basic banking products. Providing advice on loans or real estate does not require a licence.

Blurring of the advice boundaries

Advice boundaries in the Australian financial services market have become increasingly blurred through forces such as technological innovation, globalisation and industry reform.

The internet has had a dramatic effect on the whole industry, particularly stockbroking. It has made it easier for investors to buy and sell shares, but has also led to brokers' advisory services being regarded as an optional extra.

The dramatic explosion of online broking over the past decade has forced us to wonder about the future of the stockbroking industry, particularly when you consider that the largest online broker, CommSec, now accounts for more than half of the online market.

The flip side to this trend is the large and looming baby boomer generation, who will be looking to retire in the next ten years and will have more retirement savings than any generation before them. They are going to need advice.

And globalisation has broken down the historical boundaries between countries and regions of the world, allowing investors to look beyond their own shores and gain access to new markets and new investment opportunities. So investors are seeking and demanding a broader range of products and services to satisfy their needs. They expect service providers in the financial services industry to work with them to facilitate this access, whether it is in direct equities or managed funds.

In fact, it is the ordinary private investors who are forcing the financial services industry to redefine its service offerings and provide a greater scope to satisfy all of our needs, as opposed to piecemeal service provision. Many of us want a one-stop shop for all our financial needs rather than having to chase a handful of professionals located in different offices with different areas of expertise. For example, many of us want to seek out more services than a financial planner has typically provided. Yes, we may want managed funds and direct property in our investment portfolios, but we also want direct equities.

Responding to this demand, more financial planners are getting training on products such as direct equities to broaden their scope of advice and market appeal. So financial planners are now getting more involved in an industry that used to be solely the preserve of stockbrokers.

This is similar to the blurring of advice boundaries between financial planners and accountants and advice for setting up self-managed superannuation funds (SMSFs).

Historically, SMSFs were the realm of financial planners, however the regulator of these products, the Australian Taxation Office, realised that most of the SMSFs were being established by accountants.

To curb the explosion in SMSFs and to make sure investors were setting them up for the right reasons, accountants now have limited scope to provide information on SMSFs. More on this subject later.

But whose advice do we value the most? Research conducted by the Australian Stock Exchange (ASX) in 2004 found that financial planners were ranked as the number one source of information that influenced respondents' direct share decisions, equal first with newspapers and family and friends.

However, when respondents were asked their most popular source of information and advice on direct shares, financial planners were ranked third (30 per cent) behind newspapers (44 per cent) and family and friends (33 per cent). Increases in courses provided by industry associations keen to broaden their memberships and improve the skills of their members are a big factor in the blurring of the advice boundaries.

We have already mentioned that more financial planners are being trained on direct equities investing. The ASX offers financial planners specialist listed investment education to gain the appropriate skills and knowledge to advise on ASX-listed investments.

Planners have flocked to its two courses, the ASX Accredited Listed Product Adviser Program and the Listed Product Accreditation Course, recognising that investors want specialist equities advice as an integral part of their investment portfolio.

Meanwhile, CPA Australia offers its members PS146 training (training to become a financial planner).

While technology and globalisation have broadened our

capacity and ability to provide services and advice, industry reform has really set the parameters within which advice professionals can offer their services. It has perhaps had the greatest impact in blurring the boundaries between advice professions.

This is not to say that regulation and industry reform have stifled the industry, but it is a difficult thing to get right. We would all agree on the need for industry regulation to ensure consumer protection, but it is also important to ensure that the industry is not tied up in so much red tape that the cost of compliance outweighs the benefits.

The *Financial Services Reform Act* 2001 (*FSRA*)

The *Financial Services Reform Act 2001* (*FSRA*) is the most far-reaching reform package in the history of the Australian financial services industry because it was designed to bring all financial services and products under a single regulatory regime.

Commencing in 2002, the financial services industry had two years to transition to the new licensing and training requirements, an indication of the detail of the reforms. It meant that to be a provider of a financial service, you have to either hold an Australian Financial Services Licence or be authorised by an AFSL holder to provide a financial service on their behalf, as an Authorised Representative.

FSRA is often referred to as 'umbrella legislation' and has received much criticism within the industry because it does not distinguish between the services provided by different parts of the industry.

For example, under *FSRA* some stockbrokers consider they are being treated as though they are financial planners, having to demonstrate they have taken into consideration a client's circumstance and generating paperwork following each transaction that details any advice given.

This is a profession that has based itself on a dynamic, fast-changing market, where timing is everything and action needs to be instantaneous. How can such an industry respond to its clients' needs and demands if it has to operate in a way than limits the scope to act quickly?

According to the Securities and Derivatives Association's policy executive, Doug Clark, there is no evidence that the new regulations have resulted in a more informed client as there has been no increase in complaints with FICS since *FSRA*'s inception.

In a presentation to Monash University's FSR Forum, Clark notes the US experience, where since 2000 stricter requirements were introduced following the dot.com bust. He says there are now calls for a rolling back of the requirements due to a dramatic decline in the level of initial public offering (IPO) activity being instigated in the US as large global companies started choosing markets other than the US to conduct their IPOs.

Further, the application of *FSRA* reforms has not gone particularly easily in the broking industry. Thomson Australia notes there have been an estimated 4000 exemptions and modifications to *FSRA* since 2003. This is on top of the regulations that already apply to the stockbroking industry: 400 pages of Corporations Law and 300 pages of the ASX Market Rules and Listing Rules. Such regulation can not only create duplication, but also makes a complying service more expensive to adequately provide.

Under the *Corporations Act 2001*, anyone who carries on a financial services business is required to either hold an Australian Financial Services Licence or operate under one. The best way to check this is to visit the ASIC consumer website (www.fido.asic.gov.au).

It is a licensee's responsibility, among other things, to ensure its financial planners have adequate training and competence, and that they manage any conflicts of interest and conduct risk management. They also provide financial planning businesses with financial assistance including technical support, research services, marketing material and software.

If you are looking for some limited advice on a specific issue, you should probably use an accountant. For more thorough financial advice, where your personal goals have been taken into consideration, a Statement of Advice must be issued by a licensed adviser.

If you are seeking comprehensive financial advice and a financial plan, it is important to consider areas that might be important to you. These will include products and services you would like a financial planner to cover, such as direct shares or property investing, insurance, estate planning, superannuation, salary sacrificing or tax-effective investing.

Remember, not all financial planners cover all investment categories, and some specialise in particular investments. Their qualifications and the specific products they are licensed for must be listed in the Financial Services Guide on their websites.

Training requirements are a central plank of the new reform system under which financial planners operate. At a minimum, a financial planner must hold a Diploma in Financial Planning and undertake continuing professional development, such as attending conferences and workshops to keep up to date with market and industry trends.

Certified Financial Planner (CFP) is the highest designation a financial planner can hold. CFP planners are qualified with a degree, have a set period of minimum professional experience and adhere to the Financial Planning Association's (FPA) Code of Ethics and Rules of Professional Conduct. This code includes rules on disclosure, financial plan preparation and explanation, client service, complaints, education, competency and supervision. It can be viewed on the FPA website (www.fpa.asn.au).

Last year the FPA members also adopted the Principles for Managing Conflicts of Interest to help members achieve their number-one obligation: to work in the best interests of their clients. These principles cover issues such as separately identifying financial planning fees in Statements of Advice and the regular disclosure of total fees being charged to a client on an ongoing basis.

Choosing a financial planner

The questions to ask

Before asking any questions, the first step is to check that the business or person you are considering using for financial advice is licensed. ASIC maintains a register of licensed people, which can be accessed online at www.asic.gov.au/licensees, or by phone on 1300 300 630.

The first line of questioning should be aimed at exploring the experience and qualifications of the financial planner. You should also ask for details about how long the planner has been in business, the most common sort of clients they advise and whether there are any products that they do not give advice on.

Your next question should be about fees. You should get a clear explanation of fees and commissions the adviser receives, plus general explanations about any likely product fees. Don't be shy about this; you are buying a service and you need to ask the price.

Finally, you should ask how the planner keeps up to date with changes in the industry, such as attending training, and if they have any professional memberships.

Financial planners are not all the same. They vary in experience, educational standards, the way they earn their income and the way they are either licensed (or operate as an authorised representative of a dealer group).

Each of these differences will affect their ability to work with you to meet your financial needs. Being aware of all these different factors — and able to choose a person who meets your expectations — will put you in a position of strength as a consumer.

The regulator of the financial planning industry, the Australian Securities & Investments Commission, has developed the following questions it recommends investors should ask a financial planner when shopping for advice:

- How long have you been giving advice?
- What qualifications do you have?
- What kind of clients do you mostly see?
- What are your clients mostly trying to achieve?
- Do you take a special interest in a particular type of financial product?
- Are there any financial products you don't advise on?
- How do you go about understanding a new client?
- How do you deal with a client who may have conflicting objectives?
- How much is this advice likely to cost in dollars and as a percentage?
- How do you keep up to date with everything that is happening?

Stockbrokers

While shares listed on the Australian Stock Exchange can only be bought and sold through a broker, you have a choice to do this either through a full-service or non-advisory broker. The difference between the two is the provision of advice.

Full-service brokers offer advice on buying and selling shares and other securities, such as debentures, government bonds and listed property trusts. If they are accredited, they may also offer advice on options, warrants and futures. Their realm of expertise is not just limited to listed investments. They can also advise on non-listed investments and retirement planning, and provide planning, implementing and monitoring of your investment portfolio. These types of broker make recommendations to you and tailor their advice and investment plans to your needs.

As a result of this more personalised service, you generally pay higher brokerage than the average fee of 2.5 per cent or the flat rate per transaction that the online brokers charge.

Non-advisory brokers are commonly internet or telephone-based. They don't offer advice, but rather a quick mechanism to transact on the stock exchange with a minimum of fuss.

While you can gain access to shares via a pooled investment vehicle such as managed fund that invests in shares, by going direct you have more control over what stocks you buy, when you sell them and how you use the ensuing capital gains or losses. What's more, the process of investing in shares directly has become a lot easier over the past ten years. Technology has played a big part in increasing the speed and security of investing in shares, as well as reducing the costs associated with buying and selling.

Making the decision whether to use a stockbroker or go through the growing band of discount brokers really comes down to whether you need advice on what stocks to pick.

If you choose to use a full-service stockbroker, you will need to set up a trading account and a cash management trust to finance your share purchases and to receive dividends.

According to the Australian Stock Exchange, share transactions can start at $500 plus brokerage, however $2000 is a good starting point, due to the costs involved.

Brokerage fees are either a percentage of the value of the purchase or the sale, or a flat rate for online brokers. ASIC says typically the fee is 2.5 per cent, but in fact that would be the top of the range for a small trade with a full-service broker. Most percentage fees for trades of more than $15,000 or so would be less than 1 per cent, and about 0.1 per cent for trades of $1 million or more.

The best way to execute small trades of less than $10,000 is through one of the online discount brokers. Their transaction fees range from $17.99 (Netwealth, for trades of up to $5000) to $29.95 with the major banks. Commsec, the nation's largest online broker, charges $19.95 for trades up to $10,000 and $29.95 for trades up to $25,000. Above that it's 0.12 per cent.

While the discount brokers do charge lower commissions, they also have access to fewer products and you will not be able to get access to many, if any, initial public offerings, otherwise known as floats. These are still the domain of larger stockbroking houses such as ABN-Amro Morgans Limited, Macquarie Equities Limited, Ord Minnett and Shaw Stockbroking.

Here is a list of questions you should ask a stockbroker before you trade with them:

1 What type of services do you provide?
2 How do you charge for your services?
3 Will I receive a regular newsletter or information on any new sharemarket opportunities?
4 What sort of information can I obtain on your website?
5 Do you conduct client seminars?
6 Are you or your firm associated with any of the companies whose investment products are recommended by you?
7 What research facilities does the firm make use of?
8 How might you review my investment plan and how regularly would you do that? (full service brokers only)
9 Do I have to set up an account with you before I can trade? How long will this take?

Accountants

Working with an accountant can be a rewarding experience because their knowledge of tax can have a huge impact on your financial future. But it is important to recognise what accountants can and cannot advise you on in relation to your investment portfolio.

Superannuation has been a sore spot for many accountants, particularly as many of us turn to our accountants for advice. And given their intimate knowledge of our personal finances and the fact that superannuation is one of the most tax-effective investment vehicles going, this is not surprising.

But under *FSRA*, there are strict rules about the level of advice accountants can give. Unless an accountant is licensed to do so, he or she is not able to give advice about the performance of different types of superannuation choices or funds. Also, they are also not able to recommend one structure over another.

So what advice can your accountant give you about super? Accountants can provide information about the differences between superannuation products such as a retail funds and establishing, structuring and operating your own self-managed superannuation fund (SMSF). They need to keep their advice focused on the structural differences between different fund choices without making a particular recommendation.

Once you have made your own decision, an accountant can help you set up an SMSF and roll over assets into it.

CPA Australia provides a very detailed analysis of what accountants can and cannot do with regards to superannuation advice. For more information visit www.cpaaustralia.com.au.

Managed discretionary accounts

Coinciding with the blurring of boundaries between the advice professions, product development has also taken a similar direction. There is a new range of products on the market that offer a premium investment and financial planning service that includes financial advice, custody services and the ability to trade in financial products tax effectively.

Known as Managed Discretionary Account (MDA) services, these are essentially a private portfolio management service for investors with more than $100,000 to manage. They are the Rolls-Royce of investment and planning services.

The unique feature of these services is that you retain ultimate control over your investments. It is your trusted financial adviser who actually makes the day-to-day portfolio decisions on your behalf.

According to ASIC, the regulation of MDA services covers products marketed as separately managed accounts, individually managed accounts, investment advisory programs and managed discretionary portfolio services.

These products have had huge success in the US, and they have been offered in the Australian market for about five years.

Although they are mainly marketed to the wealthy end of the investor market, with minimum investment sums of $250,000, Asgard Wealth Solutions has launched the first separately managed account with a lower investment threshold; one servicing the $100,000-plus market.

MDA services are commonly offered by large financial institutions such as Macquarie Bank and Westpac, as well as financial planning groups servicing wealthy individuals.

Given that MDA services combine custody, administration and financial planning services, it is important to realise that not all providers manage all of these various components of the service themselves: they might outsource the financial advice and custody services to external providers. This must be disclosed in the Financial Services Guide.

Further, if an MDA provider does outsource any of the components of the service, it is important to understand the implications. Put simply, the MDA operator is no longer legally responsible for the outsourced service.

Providers of MDAs commonly conduct their own equities research. They actively look for new investment opportunities such as initial public offerings, a big attraction for rich people who want access to these investments as well as the tax benefits of investing in equities.

This means they should have good research departments based on great people and process. Make sure you understand what resources an MDA provider uses for its equities research.

Benefits of MDAs

MDA services combine financial advice, active portfolio management and administration services. Timely and active financial advice and management has obvious benefits for the investor. You can jump in when the investment opportunities arise and you have a professional adviser looking out for your needs around the clock. Administration services give an investor online access to their portfolio, access to shares and wholesale funds, and ongoing consolidated tax reporting.

However, the biggest advantage for an investor — and perhaps the main reason you would choose an MDA over a unit trust (and also the main reason why some investors are willing to pay more for the service) — is the ability to minimise tax.

Within an MDA, assets are held on behalf of the investor, who is able to customise their portfolio to optimise their tax position. Given that capital gains tax is halved on investments held for more than 12 months, individual investors are likely to time their buying and selling to minimise tax payable.

Pooled investment vehicles generally ignore the tax implications of their trades, which means tax liabilities are often embedded in the price of the units. And they report the more impressive pre-tax, rather than after-tax returns, so you can't properly compare their performance with an MDA.

Investors in MDAs, being treated individually, are not taxed on behalf of other investors and can take advantage of the products that should allow them to realise a loss for tax purposes if this is beneficial for their situation at any point in time.

Fees of MDAs are commonly charged as a percentage of funds under management and they are usually very expensive — often far too expensive for what you get. A tiered scale may also be applied, where the percentage decreases over various thresholds. To give you some idea, Westpac Private Portfolio Management has a minimum fee of $16,500 a year, charged on total funds under management, irrespective of the investment options.

Above $1 million under management, the fee reduces to 1.5 per cent and down to 1.35 per cent above $2 million, then 0.85 per cent for $3 million and above. This service caters for investors with at least $1 million to invest. The range on management fees for MDA services seems to range from 1.5 per cent to as high as 4 per cent.

Further, fees can also be charged on the basis of individual trades, including brokerage on share trades, options and advisory fees, which are paid monthly. Some providers charge a flat fee.

Regulation of MDAs

Providers of MDA services must comply with specific ASIC regulations. These regulations have been in place since November 2004. ASIC concludes that their product features make MDA services both a managed investment scheme and a facility for making a financial investment. This has implications on MDA providers' licensing requirements.

An MDA provider must have an Australian Financial Services Licence as well as an AFSL authorisation to deal in financial products, give financial advice and operate a custody service. Interestingly, the regulation of MDA services goes one step further than the regulation of other forms of financial advice.

Although all financial planners must demonstrate knowledge of the product and knowledge of their clients, ASIC says that MDA operators must also act in their clients' best interests, act honestly and give priority to their clients' interests.

Case study

Over three years Kevin Brown had paid nothing for the financial advice he had received, which should have sounded alarm bells. He describes the near total collapse of his finances as like that of a house of cards, as they came crashing down all at once.

Kevin Brown, 37, considers himself a pro-active investor and didn't like the idea of his money sitting idle in a bank account. So after attending a seminar organised by his accounting firm, he took out a loan to invest $250,000 in a tax-effective insurance bond scheme, which guaranteed a return of 13 per cent per annum.

After a year, the Victorian father of two realised that his initial investment had shrunk to $235,000 and relayed his concerns to his financial adviser, who explained the deduction as a tax payment.

But when an investment bank contacted him over concerns it had with the way the scheme was being administered, he withdrew the remaining funds. Two years later, the company running the scheme folded.

'They wound up the company too, so there was no possibility of tracking them down to recover our money,' said Mr Brown.

Not only did Mr Brown lose $15,000, some time later he received a $50,000 bill from the Australian Tax Office. 'The ATO ruled that the scheme was established as a deliberate loss-making venture which I wasn't aware of, but I was sure it was something my adviser would have known,' he commented.

Mr Brown also lost $26,000 in a failed gold-mining project in Queensland and a tax-effective timber plantation.

Mr Brown was aware of the risks associated with high-interest investments but thought he had just run into bad luck. So after much agonising he returned once more to his financial adviser for direction on how to invest $50,000 — but this time he was not seeking high-returns high-risk investments.

'This time I definitely didn't want risk. I wanted something that was safe and conservative,' he said.

Mr Brown made out a $50,000 cheque to Westpoint Corporation. His money disappeared in the company's $300 million collapse. Of seven investments he was encouraged to make only two were not disasters.

Mr Brown now says he placed too much trust in his adviser and should have conducted his own independent research. 'I wasn't paying anything for his services so I assumed he was receiving considerable commissions on the products he was encouraging me to invest in.'

He has lodged a complaint with the Financial Industry Complaints Service. They had yet to make a ruling at time of going to press.

Chapter 6

PLATFORMS AND WRAPS

Platforms and wraps are the fastest growing products in the financial services industry and they now dominate the way individuals invest. But in many ways they are quite insidious creatures, designed to look after the interests of advisers rather than investors. That's not to say platforms and wraps are not useful for you, it's just that they were designed by and for advisers and are more useful to them than you. Occasionally they act against your interests entirely. In this chapter we explain how they work, what's good about them and what's bad about them.

The Australian Security & Investments Commission (ASIC), which regulates these products, refers to platforms and wraps as 'Investor-Directed Portfolio Services' (IDPS). ASIC defines them by the three key features that they offer to investors:

- a custodial service that holds assets on behalf of the investor (an administrative function that 'wraps around' a portfolio of investments)
- consolidated reporting for the investor
- the investor makes decisions about their underlying investments — choosing managed investments or direct investments.

Investor-directed portfolio services, which for simplicity's sake we'll call wraps, have been the boom financial product of the past ten years. Huge fortunes have been made by the big financial services operators, mainly the banks, in running the software programs that control wraps and charging a percentage of your money for the privilege.

According to Standard & Poor's, as at the of 30 June 2006, the following wraps were the biggest in the marketplace:

Macquarie Wrap	$13.8 billion (in funds under administration)
BT Wrap (Westpac)	$12.9 billion
Colonial Group (CBA)	$6.9 billion
MLC (National Bank)	$4.7 billion
Asgard (St George Bank)	$4.1 billion

If you go to a financial planner today, you are more likely than not to have your money put into a wrap account associated with that planner, or the bank-owned 'dealer-group' the adviser works for. This will probably seem like a good idea, but it might not be, and it certainly might not be only in your interests.

ASIC, in its document entitled 'Tips on Master Trusts and Wrap Accounts', makes the point that 'master trust and wrap accounts can certainly offer convenience and savings for *advisers*'. ASIC is putting it mildly: platforms and wraps are mainly for the convenience of advisers.

Wraps are now large and profitable financial products that have been embraced by the big financial services institutions, as the figures above show. Are the recommendations to use a wrap, routinely made by financial planners licensed through large financial institutions, mainly in the interest of the profitability of these institutions?

Master trusts are mentioned in the same categories as wraps by ASIC and they are similar investment vehicles.

The difference between the two lies largely in the portability of the underlying investments. A platform or wrap is a custodial service. This means they hold the investments on behalf of the investor. It is possible to transfer investments from one wrap (custodial service) to another. By comparison, a master trust offers a number of wholesale funds that are unique to that master trust. Investors are not able to transfer their investments in the master trust without selling them. Being able to transfer the investments in a wrap, an investor is able to move their underlying investments between wraps without incurring capital gains tax.

Wraps are available for investments held in a person's own name, as well as for superannuation investments, where the wrap also performs the function of a superannuation trustee (usually for an additional cost). Superannuation wraps, however, do not offer the ability to transfer investments capital gains tax-free between wraps because changing the wrap means changing the trustee of the superannuation account, triggering a capital gains tax event.

The issue of fees is always the most important one for an investor. With platforms or wraps there are layers of fees that are collected — or skimmed — from your account and these need to be carefully considered before you buy the service. These fees range from entry fees and transaction fees, to the administrative fee charged by the wrap, to the advice fee collected by the financial planner. They are detailed later in this chapter.

As well as the fees that an adviser is able to smoothly take from an account through a wrap, a recommendation to use one is often as much for the adviser's convenience as the client's. For an adviser, a wrap means that:

• There is usually only one application form required to set up a portfolio, rather than multiple application forms. This makes means significantly less paperwork in setting up a client portfolio.

- Client portfolios are all in the one place, so an adviser can easily monitor the portfolio. When it comes time to review the portfolio, or send out reports for the portfolio, this is very easy for the adviser if the investments are all in the one place.
- Platforms or wraps provide the financial planner with the ability to transact easily on a client's portfolio.
- The wrap is a very efficient way of collecting client fees, whether it is through trailing commissions from products or through the collection of an adviser fee on top of the existing wrap fees.

This is the basis for the earlier ASIC comment that 'wrap accounts certainly offer convenience and savings for advisers'. In other words, wraps have been invented to make the financial advisers' lives easier, but you pay for them ... and keep paying.

Benefits of a wrap

But don't get us wrong; wraps can benefit consumers and your financial adviser will certainly list them when proposing that you put all of your money into his one. They include the following.

- Your investments are all in the one place (and one account).
- You receive consolidated reporting and regular updates.
- You can build a well-diversified portfolio with the investment choices available within a wrap.
- You are able to access cheaper, wholesale funds.
- There are usually a range of transaction options (such as regular investments, regular withdrawals and automatic rebalancing of the portfolio).

- The wrap may provide trustee responsibilities (in the case of a superannuation fund).

Let's look at each of these benefits in turn, and think about the value that's added for the investor by each of them.

All your investments in one place

It's true: using a wrap means that your total investment portfolio is in the one place: the one investment account. This means that an investor has one account number and one point of inquiry for all investments related to the account.

How much value does this add? Well, even though this makes account-keeping 'tidier' for the investor, it's hardly a unique or valuable service. Most stockbrokers, both online and full-service, have systems for investors to log on and view their holdings. So for direct shares the benefit of having all the investments in the one place exists already through this online facility. Many fund managers also provide online access for their investors. Super funds, which are an alternative to a wrap account, also provide consolidated performance reviews as well.

Consolidated reporting

Consolidated reporting means that rather than receiving individual reports and updates on each of the investments in the portfolio, the investor receives one complete report that covers the overall portfolio.

Perhaps the most important of these reports is the consolidated tax report. This provides a summary of all of the capital gains tax, dividends, income and interest received in the portfolio. This tax report saves an investor having to collect all of the dividend statements, interest statements, managed fund statements and cash statements over the year.

Regular updates

Generally, consolidated reporting also provides regular updates on the portfolio, perhaps quarterly. These regular reports will include comments on the performance of the portfolio, the investments held in the portfolio and the asset allocation of the portfolio.

On an ongoing basis investors are able to log in to their portfolio, see the holdings of the portfolio at any time, and generate reports on the portfolio.

These reports provide a regular and constant update on the performance of the portfolio. That said, most other investment options, such as investing directly into managed funds or shares, provide easy access to managed fund unit prices and share prices, so it should not be difficult for an investor to track the performance of their portfolio without the use of a wrap.

The consolidated tax report makes an investor's job easier by reducing the amount of paperwork that has to be collected over the year.

Diversification and choice

Most platforms and wraps will advertise that they offer a range of investments available for investors. Some offer hundreds of managed funds and the choice often extends to investments listed on the Australian Stock Exchange. This allows the investor to build a well diversified portfolio using the investment options within a wrap, including investments from different asset classes, in their portfolio.

How much value does this add? Investors have a large choice of investment options without having to use a wrap. You can access direct share investments, listed investment companies and a huge range of managed funds directly. There may be a small amount of choice added for an investor with access to some boutique fund managers or wholesale fund managers. This will be particularly true for investors with small amounts of money; they will be able to access more choice using a wrap.

And as we explain elsewhere in this book, diversification is one of the most misunderstood and misused concepts in the investment world. You simply don't need hundreds of managed funds to get sufficient diversity in your investments; 20 different listed companies or a handful of well-chosen fund managers is plenty.

Wholesale funds

The ability to access lower-cost wholesale funds is regularly trumpeted as a key benefit of wraps.

How much value does this add? Most investors can't access wholesale funds unless they have minimum investment amounts ranging from $25,000 through to $1 million. Wraps do allow most investors access to lower-cost wholesale funds. But the whole point about accessing lower-cost wholesale funds is to save money on fees. However, in using a wrap, you are adding another layer of fees to your portfolio. Therefore this will only add value to your situation if the total of the wholesale managed fund fee and the wrap fee is less than the fee you would pay in the equivalent retail managed fund.

Range of options

While each platform or wrap will be different, there are usually a range of transaction options, such as regular investments, regular withdrawals and automatic rebalancing of the portfolio. These functions will include such things as:

- regular investments, where additional portfolio contributions are made on a regular basis, and invested automatically in a preset investment portfolio
- dollar cost averaging, where regular investments from the cash account are made into the other investments in the portfolio

- automatic rebalancing of the account, where the asset allocation of the portfolio is automatically adjusted if it moves outside of a preset range.

Automating transaction options such as regular investments means that, for an investor, the transactions will be done without any additional effort. The value of this for an investor is the ability to set a plan, such as investing a regular monthly amount into an agreed portfolio, and have that plan carried out automatically. For those who have little time or are just plain lazy, this is probably a worthwhile benefit.

Trustee responsibilities

The benefit of 'trustee responsibility' refers to a wrap operating as a superannuation wrap that performs the trustee responsibilities of the superannuation fund. This includes calculating the superannuation tax, accepting contributions, keeping track of the various superannuation components of a person's balance and calculating and paying any pension payments.

It may offer a way for an investor to have greater control over their superannuation assets without having to take on the trustee responsibilities and high fixed costs that come with a self-managed super fund. If, for example, an investor has $100,000 in a wrap that charges a fee of 1 per cent, the $1000 annual fee will be considerably less than the yearly $2000 to $2500 of the average self-managed super fund.

The wrap will provide the investor with a significant amount of investment choice and control, with most wraps allowing investors access to both managed-fund investments and stock-exchange-listed investments.

The value for investors is explained below. It is possible that a wrap would allow an investor with a moderate superannuation balance ($50,000 to $200,000) a good deal of control over their superannuation investments at a much lower cost than a self-managed super fund.

Self-managed super funds versus wraps

There is no doubting the rise and rise of the self-managed superannuation fund (SMSF) as an investment vehicle. It provides investors with a level of control over their superannuation assets previously unavailable. The cost of this control is that the members of SMSFs have to accept trustee responsibilities for their fund. It is very clear that regardless of the advisers and accountants who are assisting them with their SMSF, the buck stops with the fund's trustees to maintain an appropriate investment strategy, following the rules relating to operating an SMSF and ensuring that audits and tax returns are carried out and lodged on time. This is a considerable amount of responsibility for a trustee of an SMSF, which often becomes more onerous as people age.

An alternative is the use of a wrap. Most wraps and platforms allow a wide enough range of investments that a portfolio built in an SMSF could also be built in a wrap. Most platforms offer a very wide range of managed funds, from low-cost passive funds through to boutique funds, and many offer access to ASX-listed securities including Australian shares, fixed-interest securities, listed investment companies and listed property trusts.

The benefit of using a wrap is that its operators assume the trustee responsibilities. The individual investor doesn't have to worry about audits, super fund tax returns, appropriate rules of pension payments or investment strategies; the wrap does all of this. It will also calculate your pension payments, if you are retired, and make these payments to you.

It is important not to forget that this convenience comes at a cost. If a $250,000 SMSF costs $2000 a year to operate, and the equivalent wrap, at 2 per cent, costs $5000 a year, this is a very significant cost difference and must be considered when choosing between the two. The costs of an SMSF are generally fixed, regardless of the size of the fund. Wraps always charge a percentage-based fee, meaning the fee increases with the size of the portfolio.

That would suggest that for larger superannuation funds, an SMSF would be more cost-effective, as the fixed cost of the fund won't increase with the size of the fund. Many wraps offer a tiered fee scheme, reducing the percentage as the portfolio grows. For example, the Macquarie Super Wrap charges a fee of 0.77 per cent on the initial $50,000 of each investment option held in the wrap, and 0.1 per cent on the amount of each additional investment above $50,000.

At the moment wraps do not allow investors to hold 'non-traditional' investments such as business, real estate, artwork or direct property investments. SMSFs offer the flexibility that allows investors access to these assets within their superannuation fund, subject to the investment rules that govern superannuation.

Disadvantages of wraps

The negatives of using a wrap have to be considered alongside the positives. The two key negatives are:

- the fees
- the fact that a financial planner's recommendation to use a wrap may be more in their own interest, or that of the financial services institution that they work for, than the client's.

Fees

Most platforms or wraps have a number of layers of fees associated with them. These include:

- The investment manager fees — the fees charged by the underlying investment managers. They range from no fee for investments in stock exchange-listed securities through to over 2 per cent for retail managed funds.
- The administration fee — charged by the wrap for the administration of the investor account. This is usually the most significant fee, ranging from 0.5–1.5 per cent. Quite often this is a tiered-type fee, meaning that it decreases for larger portfolio balances.
- The adviser fee — charged by the financial planner. This is usually a variable fee that can be altered for each client. It often contains an up-front and an ongoing component, and may be either a flat dollar fee or a percentage-based fee.
- The trustee fee — similar to the administration fee, it is charged by a superannuation wrap for taking on the role of superannuation trustee.
- Transaction fees— charged on each transaction within the wrap. For example, if you buy or sell a managed fund within the investment account, a fee will be charged for the transaction.
- 'Shelf-space' fees — an important fee to be aware of in understanding how wraps operate. Such a fee is paid from a fund manager to a wrap for being included as part of the wrap. This is another fee that should concern investors because it potentially interferes with the independence of the wrap. Shelf-space fees might cause investors to ask whether the investment is part of the platform or wrap because it is the best investment available, or because it was prepared to pay more shelf-space fees?

The contentious thing about wraps
Are they mainly in the interest of clients, financial planners or financial service institutions?

In this chapter we have looked at the value created by wraps for individual investors and have found that there can be value for clients. This value comes at a price and this price means that wraps may not be the best option for everybody. If you find yourself sitting opposite a financial planner who is recommending a wrap for your investment portfolio, you need to keep in mind that the recommendation is likely to benefit them and the financial institution that they happen to work for — possibly more than it will benefit you.

From the perspective of a financial planner, wraps offer a simple way of managing, transacting on and reviewing client portfolios. Wraps allow the easy collection of client fees through an adviser fee charged on the portfolio and/or through trailing commissions from the managed investments recommended in the portfolio or the wrap itself. As well as the commissions from the wrap or investments, financial planners may also receive a rebate from the wrap itself, based on placing a certain volume of business. All in all, this provides the basis of an attractive business model for financial planners: easy-to-manage client portfolios with easy-to-collect business revenue.

A look at a recent Westpac annual report shows how important wraps have become for financial institutions. The 2006 report shows that BT, Westpac's wealth management business, has $1.4 billion more funds under administration (held in a wrap or similar) than funds under management (their funds management business). The report says that 'the success of our wrap and corporate super businesses ... drove an 11 per cent rise in fee income'. Two paragraphs before this, shareholders are told that 'solid growth in funds under administration' is attributed, in part, to 'solid growth in planner numbers and productivity'. It is not difficult to join the dots. From a corporate perspective, at Westpac larger numbers of more productive financial planners are helping to grow their successful wrap business by recommending it to clients.

For financial planners and financial institutions alike, wraps provide the ability to be more independent from the underlying managed fund investments, while still recommending and distributing an investment product — the wrap — that is very much in their own interest.

It is not unreasonable to suggest that this apparent move away from financial planners being managed funds salespeople for big financial institutions is in the best interest of clients. However, the fact that managed funds are replaced by a fee-producing administrative structure in the wrap simply replaces one conflict of interest with another.

Are wraps for everyone?

The short answer to this question is no. Not everyone will be suited to using a wrap for their investment portfolio. Indeed there seems to be quite a variance in the usefulness of a wrap, depending simply on whether the investments are held within superannuation or not.

For investments within superannuation, a wrap potentially offers an excellent alternative, or possibly a stepping-stone to an SMSF. Very few financial commentators suggest that SMSFs are cost-effective for investors with less than $200–250,000. Below this, a wrap offers investors the potential for greater control over their superannuation investments without the fixed costs and trustee responsibilities associated with an SMSF. With choice of superannuation available to many workers, a wrap allows them to take more control of the investment of their super. As the super balance grows, the assets can be transferred to an SMSF. If a transfer is made, capital gains tax will have to be paid on the investment growth in the portfolio. Assuming that the investments have been held for more than 12 months, the growth would be taxed at a discounted rate of 10 per cent.

For investments held outside superannuation, weighing up the advantages of a wrap is more difficult. The three questions that an investor has to answer for themselves are:

- Are there genuine cost savings with the wrap?
- Does the wrap offer access to investments I cannot access elsewhere?
- How much value do I put on the consolidated reporting and convenience of a wrap?

The first question is important. If an investor is considering buying a parcel of ASX-listed shares, which have no ongoing costs, then holding this portfolio in a wrap that charges 1 per cent a year actually increases the cost of the portfolio by 1 per cent a year or, alternatively, reduces the return by that amount.

Cost savings may come about where an investor wishes to access wholesale managed funds, which may be more than 1 per cent cheaper than the retail managed funds. Here, paying a 1 per cent wrap fee might actually save the investor money.

There are occasions where specialist managed investments can only be accessed through wraps. If an investor particularly wants to hold these investments in their portfolio, then clearly a wrap is necessary for at least these investments.

There is no doubt wraps provide convenience for investors in the form of consolidated tax statements, having investments in one account and having the wrap undertake the custodial responsibilities. The investor still has to put a value on that service, and decide whether it is worth the money. If they have a $100,000 portfolio of ASX-listed shares, a wrap that charges a fee of 1 per cent a year will cost the investor $1000 to use the service. The investor might prefer to forgo the convenience of a wrap and instead collect and deal with their own paperwork, saving the$1000 wrap fee in the process.

The last comment for an investor weighing up the value of a wrap is that it may make sense to have some investments in a wrap, and some outside. For an investor holding their portfolio in their own name, they may be best served holding their ASX-listed investments outside a wrap with some wholesale or specialist managed funds within a wrap.

The alternatives

The first viable alternative for investors is to take care of the paperwork themselves and track the performance of their own portfolio. A simple Microsoft Excel spreadsheet can prove to be very efficient in tracking the performance of a portfolio over time. When considering this option, bear in mind that wraps have only recently been available for investors. Before they came along people managed to keep track of their portfolios without them.

For people holding ASX-listed investments, through either an online or full-service broker, it is most likely that there will be an online option to view the value of your account and transactions. This provides a simple way of keeping up to date with your listed investments.

Many managed funds offer online access to your account, which can show you the up-to-date position of your portfolio. Even those managed funds that don't offer this will have up-to-date unit prices, so you can still follow the progress of your account without the need for a wrap.

If you opt not to use a wrap, you will have to collect the paperwork relating to all of the income and capital gains from your investments. For a portfolio of 30 investments this might amount to 60 statements over the course of a year, based on an average of two per investment. Provided you have a reasonable filing system, this should not be too onerous.

The second viable alternative to a wrap for investors is the use of portfolio-tracking software. In this case the onus is still on the investor to collect the actual paperwork for the portfolio; however, the software assists in the tracking of the portfolio. Quicken is a popular example of this type of software.

Another alternative is the 'virtual wrap' released by Praemium, an online administrative service that focuses on providing a high quality of tax reporting for portfolios, including the provision of tax summaries for both income tax and capital gains tax. The Praemium service does not actually operate a custodial service for clients, instead focusing on providing administrative and tax reporting for the portfolio. Praemium is a wholesale product but there are several retail licensees that offer it directly to investors. These are listed on our website (www.eurekaway.com.au).

Are wraps available directly?

It is possible to invest directly into many wraps instead of via a financial planner. Netwealth and Stanford Securities are examples of wrap providers that encourage investors who don't want to invest through a financial planner.

At the end of the day the best way to approach wraps, as either an investor or a client of the financial planning industry, is to be forewarned. There is no doubt that wraps offer value to clients through their consolidated reporting functions and their ability for investors to access lower-cost wholesale funds or investments with significantly higher minimum entry amounts than they could otherwise afford. That value comes at a cost, and weighing the cost against the value is the only criterion an investor should use to work out whether a wrap service would suit them. Investors should also bear in mind that they don't have to take an 'all-or-nothing' approach to using a wrap. It might be suitable for part of their portfolio, and not for the remainder.

Case study

It was a friendship which grew steadily over 25 years of professional association, but in the end it cost Barry Hill nearly three quarters of a million dollars.

Upon retirement, Mr Hill decided to sell his New South Wales business. As he had many times before, he turned to his long-time financial planner for advice.

The financial planner advised the retiree to invest $733 000 in four property developments. These included just over $480 000 in two Westpoint Properties projects located in Sydney and Melbourne.

The 64 year old says the financial planner told him there was no risk. 'His exact words were they were "safe as a bank". Particularly because so many of the apartments had already been sold'.

The adviser gave his client literature which rated the investments 'Triple A'.

'I repeatedly told him I wanted conservative investments. I was retiring and I didn't want to go into high risk things. At our age, we don't want to risk everything. He kept telling me Westpoint was paying good interest, there were no charges and a good payout.

'I didn't do any research myself — I completely trusted him. Besides, he'd worked for us for more than 20 years and I considered him a personal friend.'

Mr Hill believes the adviser earned $95,000 in commissions from these investments alone.

When it became publicly known the Westpoint projects were experiencing difficulties, the planner called Mr Hill to warn him there were problems with one of the projects, but said he shouldn't believe what he'd read in the paper. He said the other development was still progressing well. Within three months, Westpoint Properties had collapsed. Along with the other property investments made on his behalf which also failed, Barry Hill had lost nearly three quarters of a million dollars.

Mr Hill says he feels his financial planner betrayed him by taking advantage of their personal relationship.

'All he was concerned with was how much money he could make for himself, not our friendship. He had to have known there were concerns about Westpoint. I've since found out there were concerns about that group a lot earlier. I just can't believe somebody who'd been in the financial industry for that long didn't know about those problems. He must have known. He should lose his licence.'

The adviser is continuing to operate as a financial planner, while a long established and conservative company is advising Mr Hill: 'I'm getting lower returns, but at least I'll sleep at night.'

He says in some ways he was lucky. 'I've still got my house and I didn't need to go on the pension.'

Barry Hill holds little hope of seeing his money again, although he has joined a class action in a bid to recover some of his investment. 'Maybe the kids will see it,' he says wryly.

Chapter 7

MANAGED FUNDS

Managed funds have long been the cornerstone of the financial services industry — and to some extent, the cornerstone of what's wrong with it. They happily extracted large percentage-based fees from investors, paid fat trailing commissions to the financial planners who recommended them and avoided drawing attention to their poor performance.

This chapter takes a close look at managed funds, and starts by looking at what managed funds are and how the industry is structured. We then look at listed investment companies, a close relative of managed funds, before considering the positives and negatives of managed funds. A lot of investment theory discussion is focused on whether active or passive investment management is the best approach, and this discussion is reviewed in this chapter. We also look at some specific types of managed investments, including hedge funds and private equity funds, and the managed fund 'rating companies' that provide the research that financial planners use to justify their managed fund recommendations.

What are managed funds?

A managed funds is an investment vehicle in which a professional investment manager invests funds collectively on behalf of a large number of investors.

When a person invests in a managed fund, they are issued with a number of units in that fund. For example, a person investing $1000 in a managed fund with a unit price of $1 will receive 1000 units in the fund. If the value of the investments held in the managed fund goes up, the unit price will increase. Conversely, if the investments fall in value, the unit price will go down.

As well as investors receiving a return on their investment because of changes in the unit price, most managed funds pay distributions, often once or twice a year. These are made up of the income that has been received from the investments of the managed fund, plus any capital gains from assets that have been sold. For example, a managed fund made up of Australian shares will have received dividends from holding those shares over the year. At the end of June (effectively the end of the financial year) the managed fund will pay the value of the dividends to the unit holders in the form of a distribution.

The bottom line is that the experience of an investor in a managed fund will closely follow the performance of the investment assets of the managed fund. If the underlying investment assets perform well, the managed fund will also perform well, and vice versa.

Managed funds can either invest in a single asset class, such as Australian shares, or in multiple asset classes. A 'balanced' managed fund might invest in a range of asset classes, including Australian shares, international shares, listed property trusts, fixed interest investments and cash investments within the one fund.

Of course, the professional investment manager does not provide his services pro bono, usually charging a fee of 1.8–2.5 per cent for a 'retail' managed fund. 'Wholesale' managed funds, which require larger investments, are often much cheaper than retail managed funds, usually around 0.6–1.3 per cent. This fee is paid out of the assets of the managed fund directly to the fund manager.

The amount of money needed to access a retail managed fund is usually small, with a number of funds accepting initial contributions as small as $1000. Most wholesale funds require at least $50,000, although some have recently reduced their minimum investment to $10,000

Structure of the managed funds industry

The managed fund industry in Australia is huge. According to statistics published on the website of US managed funds industry site, the Investment Company Institute, Australia has the fourth-biggest managed fund industry in the world, ranking behind the US, France and Luxembourg but ahead of financial heavyweights such as Germany, the UK and Japan. At the start of 2006 the value of the assets invested in Australian managed funds was just over $800 billion. Given Australia's population of 20 million, that equates to $40,000 invested in managed funds for every man, woman and child in Australia.

There are more than 9000 managed funds available in Australia. To put this in perspective, at the start of 2006 there were 1873 listed companies on the Australian Stock Exchange. Sure, not all the managed funds will be invested in Australian stocks, but the fact that there are five times as many managed funds in Australia as there are listed companies on the ASX is a testament to the size of the industry.

The total value of investments listed on the ASX at the end of 2005 was $1110 billion. With $800 billion invested through managed funds (63 per cent of the value of ASX investments) it is easy to recognise the significance of the managed fund industry.

Why is this so? First, Australia's mandatory superannuation system means 9 per cent of all salaries are invested, primarily into managed funds via super funds, providing an ongoing stream of contributions. Second, Australia's financial planning industry is dominated by advisers who generate their cash flow from the commissions paid by managed funds to them. They have an inherent bias toward recommending managed funds ahead of all other types of investments, such as direct shares or property.

As discussed earlier, these commissions come in two forms: up-front and trailing. Up-front commissions can range up to 5 per cent, with trailing commissions most commonly in the range of 0.5–1 per cent. These trailing commissions are often more valuable to a financial planner than up-front commissions, as they pay an income stream to the planner every year the investment is in place. Many financial planners and discount managed fund brokers are happy to rebate the up-front commission, as long as they keep receiving the trailing commission.

Listed investment companies

Listed investment companies (LICs) can be considered a close relative of managed funds. LICs are ASX-listed companies carrying on the business of managing an investment portfolio. Investing in an LIC means that you become part-owner of the underlying investment portfolio (and the investment manager's skill). This is very similar to what you get as an investor in a managed fund.

Listed investment companies are some of the cheapest managed investments available. For example Argo, a long-established LIC that manages an Australian share portfolio, has a management fee of 0.15 per cent of the company's portfolio and Australian Foundation Investments and Carlton Investments have management fees of 0.12 per cent. These are more than ten times cheaper than the average retail managed fund fee of just over 1.8 per cent. The performance of these LICs has also been strong, with the five-year annual return to 30 September 2006, being 18.1 per cent a year for Argo, 17.96 per cent for Australian Foundation Investments and 24.62 per cent a year for Carlton Investments.

The combined market value of LICs in Australia is about 2.5 per cent of the total value of managed funds — a tiny fraction of the managed investment industry. Even though many LICs are very low cost, have excellent performance histories and have similar characteristics to managed funds, they occupy a much smaller position on the Australian investment landscape. This is largely due to the fact that managed funds pay a commission to financial advisers who recommend them, and LICs do not.

Arguments for managed funds

There are number of arguments for using managed funds. These include:

- the expertise of the fund manager
- diversification
- the ability to access 'difficult-to-access' asset classes
- the ability to set up a simple, regular investment program
- liquidity and simplicity.

Expertise

When you invest in a managed fund, the person managing your money is a full-time investment professional. Having them manage your investments means that you are accessing their expertise. The flipside to the expertise of a fund manager is the generally high cost of managed funds, with the key question for investors being whether the professional management of a managed fund increase the returns enough to outweigh the costs. The next section, looking at the negatives of managed funds, comments on the difficulties that managed fund have in overcoming these high fees.

Diversity

A single managed-fund investment provides access to a well-diversified underlying portfolio. An investment into an Australian share fund, for example, might provide access to a well-diversified portfolio of 50 companies or more. Taking this even further, an investment in a balanced managed fund provides diversification across a broad range of asset classes and investments. This is particularly beneficial for investors starting out with a small amount of money. There is no way to directly build a well-diversified portfolio of 50 Australian companies with a $2000 initial investment, while an investment in a managed fund does provide this diversification.

Difficult-to-access assets

There are many asset classes it is difficult for an investor to access. Investments in international shares, private equity and overseas property are difficult to make directly as an individual, but much easier to make through a managed fund.

Regular investing

Often managed funds allow an investor to set up an initial investment and regular additional investments. These additional investments are often referred to as 'dollar cost averaging'. They are an extremely effective way to invest because if asset prices fall you are continuing to invest more money at lower prices. The additional investment programs of managed funds can be as simple as making an initial investment of $1000 with additional investments of $100 a month. Without using managed funds it is almost impossible to make effective regular investments as small as $100 a month.

Liquidity and simplicity

The liquidity and administrative simplicity of managed funds are another advantage. It is usually only a matter of days for a managed fund investment to be sold and returned to the investor as cash. From an administrative perspective, the managed fund provides a consolidated tax statement at the end of each year and it is easy to follow the performance of the managed fund through the fund manager's website. There is no need to worry about investment decisions, as these are all made for you by the fund manager.

Arguments against managed funds

With the benefits of managed funds outlined above, and a fleet of commission-based financial planners promoting them, you could be forgiven for thinking that they are the answer to every investment problem. This is not the case, and there are arguments against using managed funds, which include:

- cost
- tax issues
- they're often too big
- they are often poor performers.

Cost

The average cost of a retail managed fund is 1.8–2 per cent a year. The long-term average return from the stockmarket has been 12–14 per cent a year. A fee of 1.8–2 per cent is equal to about 15 per cent of the overall return. This is a large part of your annual returns to be giving away in fees each year

Although a fee of 1.8–2 per cent does not sound too big, on a portfolio of $200,000 it means $3600 to $4000 a year, which is quite a chunk.

Tax inefficiency

The majority of managed funds are managed with little or no concern for the tax situation of the individual investor. Very few managed funds report their after-tax returns. This is a concern, as it is only the after-tax returns that stay in an investor's pocket. The most common tax problem for investors is the level of trading in managed funds. Sometimes more than 100 per cent of the value of the fund's assets are traded each year, which creates capital gains tax obligations for the investor.

Size

The volume of money managed by the largest fund managers is significant. The largest fund managers in Australia measure their 'funds under management' in tens of billions of dollars. Managing such large amounts of money provides three problems for fund managers.

First, when they are buying and selling stock, they purchase or sell such large quantities that they move the markets against themselves. For example, if a large fund manager wants to buy $100 million of stock in a company, because of the sheer size of the order the principles of supply and demand will push up the price of the stock they are buying.

Second, the fund manager has so much money to look after that once they invest in companies they regard as outstanding, there is still more money to invest. They then have to put money into companies that they see as 'good' and perhaps some into companies they see as 'sound'.

Third, similar to the second problem, fund managers with large volumes of money to invest are forced to put more money into the very big companies because they have a greater number of shares available, and can only put smaller amounts of money into smaller companies. The volume of money they have forces them to mainly invest in large companies and limits their ability to effectively invest in smaller companies.

Poor performance

In the majority of cases, managed funds fail the 'show me the money' test — they fail to beat the average market return, as measured by the market index.

Academic research has for quite some time identified this inability of managed funds to add value over the average market return.

For example, two economics professors from the University of Queensland, Michael Drew and Jon Stanford, examined returns from superannuation investments. In a paper published in the September 2003 edition of the *Service Industry Journal* entitled 'Returns from Investing in Australian Equity Superannuation Funds, 1991–1999', they found that 'the average superannuation fund, specialising in the management of domestic share portfolios, underperforms passive market indices by about 2.8–4 per cent per annum'. Their overall conclusion was 'Australian superannuation investors would achieve their retirement income objectives more rapidly by engaging a low-cost fund manager employing a passive technique (i.e., indexing) ...'

In his paper 'Measuring the True Cost of Active Management by Mutual (managed) Funds', American finance professor Dr Ross Miller considered the returns from 152 managed funds from January 2002 to December 2004. On an overall basis, the 152 mutual funds underperformed the index by an average of 1.5 per cent.

Russ Wermers, a finance professor at the University of Maryland wrote a paper entitled 'Mutual Fund Performance: An Empirical Decomposition into Stock-Picking Talent, Style, Transaction Costs, and Expenses' that was published in *Journal of Finance* in 2000. He found that while fund managers had some ability to select stocks that outperformed the market, the funds still underperformed the index, primarily because of expenses and transaction costs associated with an actively managed fund. This finding is significant, as it demonstrates that even in the presence of investment skill the inefficiency of managed funds meant the investor ended up with below-average investment returns. This study only looked at before-tax returns. The better-performing funds considered in Wermers' study had a portfolio turnover rate higher than 100 per cent; that is, they bought and sold their entire portfolio every year. This high level of trading would have meant higher taxes and reduced after-tax returns for the investors in these funds.

The following table is taken from an article published in Alan Kohler's 'Eureka Report' in August 2006. It looks at the investment returns achieved by fund managers listed in the ASX 100 stock exchange index. These fund managers were chosen because, being among the biggest in Australia, it was assumed that they would be the best resourced and therefore able to provide value for investors. The overall results for these funds were poor, with most unable to match the index return during the five-year period to 30 June 2006 of 12.31 per cent a year. The table has three columns for each fund: the first shows the funds' actual five-year performance; the second shows the underperformance or overperformance of the fund for this period compared with the index; and the third shows the value created or destroyed by the fund, compared to an investment in the index over this period, assuming a starting portfolio balance of $100,000.

How the funds performed

Fund	5-year annual returns to 30.6.06	5-year under or overperformance	Value created/ destroyed on $100k investment
Index return	12.31%		
AMP Limited			
AMP Equity Fund*	10.80%	−1.51%	−$7,325
AMP Blue Chip Fund*	10.70%	−1.61%	−$7,795
ANZ			
ING Australian Share Trust	11.07%	−1.24%	−$6,048
AXA Asia Pacific Holdings Limited			
AXA Equity Imputation Fund	9.10%	−3.21%	−$15,052
AXA Australian Equity Growth Fund	9.30%	−3.01%	−$14,171
AXA Industrial Fund	8.90%	−3.41%	−$15,926
Commonwealth Bank of Australia			
Colonial Australian Share Fund	10.20%	−2.11%	−$10,114
Colonial Imputation Fund	10.11%	−2.20%	−$10,527
Macquarie Bank Limited			
Macquarie Leaders Imputation Trust	10.15%	−2.16%	−$10,343
Macquarie Active Australian Equity Trust	9.17%	−3.14%	−$14,745
National Australia Bank Limited			
MLC Vanguard Australian Shares Index*	11.03%	−1.28%	−$6,238
MLC Australian Share Fund*	10.10%	−2.21%	−$10,572
Perpetual Limited			
Perpetual Industrial Share Fund	12.20%	−0.11%	−$549
St George Bank Limited			
Advance Imputation Fund	9.28%	−3.03%	−$14,259
Suncorp-Metway Limited			
Suncorp Australian Shares Fund	12.83%	0.52%	$2,627
Westpac Banking Corporation			
BT Australian Share Fund	11.14%	−1.17%	−$5,715
BT Imputation Fund	14.88%	2.57%	$13,528
Average	**10.64%**	**−1.67%**	**−$8,054**

* 5 year returns to 31 May 2006

The following table is taken from an article published in Alan Kohler's 'Eureka Report' in February 2007. It looks at the investment returns that have been achieved by fund managers who are listed in the ASX 100 stock exchange index. These fund managers were chosen because, being among the biggest in Australia, it was assumed that they would be the best resourced and therefore able to provide value for investors. The overall results for these funds was poor, with most unable to match the index return during the 1, 3 or 5-year period to the end of December 2006. The top row of returns shows the ASX 300 index return to the end of December 2006.

The table has three columns for each fund. They compare the 1-year, 3-year and 5-year returns with the index. The very bottom row shows the average underperformance by the funds over each time period – underperforming the index by 2.89% and 1.89% a year. This is a weak result.

The table highlights the few times that managed funds have actually beaten the index.

How the managed funds performed

Returns to end of December, 2006	1-year return (%)	3-year average annual return (%)	5-Year average annual return (%)
ASX 300 Index Return (accumulation)	24.51	24.94	15.42
AMP Limited			
AMP Equity Fund	20.80	23.50	12.90
AMP Blue Chip Fund	20.30	23.20	12.80
Australia and New Zealand Banking Group Limited			
ING Australian Share Trust	19.85	22.32	13.27
ING Blue Chip Imputation Trust	20.19	20.85	12.76
AXA Asia Pacific Holdings Limited			
AXA Equity Imputation Fund	22.60	25.10	12.90
AXA Australian Equity Growth Fund	22.50	24.70	12.60
Challenger Financial Services Group Limited			
Challenger Australian Share Fund	23.55	24.31	16.55

Returns to end of December, 2006	1-year return (%)	3-year average annual return (%)	5-Year average annual return (%)
Commonwealth Bank of Australia			
Colonial Australian Share Fund	19.18	22.32	12.79
Colonial Imputation Fund	20.36	22.59	12.66
Macquarie Bank Limited			
Macquarie Leaders Imputation Trust	19.32	22.31	12.25
Macquarie Active Aust Equity Trust	20.23	22.47	11.56
National Australia Bank Limited			
MLC Vanguard Aust Shares Index	22.30	23.10	13.80
MLC Australian Share Fund	22.30	23.10	13.80
Perpetual Limited			
Perpetual Industrial Share Fund	21.30	21.10	15.20
St George Bank Limited			
Advance Imputation Fund	17.63	17.78	11.05
Advance Sharemarket Fund	20.39	20.55	13.10
Suncorp-Metway Limited			
Suncorp Australian Shares Fund	26.38	25.69	15.96
Westpac Banking Corporation			
BT Australian Share Fund	22.70	24.56	14.17
BT Imputation Fund	28.83	28.11	18.04
Average return	**21.62**	**23.03**	**13.59**
Average underperformance	**– 2.89**	**– 1.91**	**– 1.83**

Active versus passive investing

One of the big debates related to investing is whether investment managers should use an active or passive approach.

An active investment approach is the most commonly adopted. Fund managers use their expertise to try and pick investments, such as shares, that will outperform the average investment return — the index return. An active approach doesn't mean the investment manager is trading all the time, just that they are taking specific positions with the intent of beating the average market return.

A passive investment approach means an investor does not try to beat the market, rather they accept the market return by investing through an 'index fund'.

An index is a collection of all the investments in an investment category. It is used to measure the overall performance of all the investments in that category. For example, the index of the largest 200 companies listed on the ASX is known as the ASX 200 index. It measures the average performance of the largest 200 companies by value. As we write, the value of the ASX 200 index is about 5000 points. In any one day the index may go up by 50 points (1 per cent) if the average value of the companies in the index rises by 1 per cent. Alternately, if the average value of the companies falls then the index will fall.

Most indices are value weighted, which means that larger companies have more importance in the index. In Australia this is true. In the ASX 200 index, companies such as BHP Billiton, the major banks and Telstra have more weight in the index, so changes in their price will influence the index more than changes in the prices of smaller companies.

Indices were set up as measuring devices. Once research was done that looked at the investment performance of active managers it was noticed that very few active fund managers could beat the index over any extended period.

In the early 1970s in the United States, the first 'index fund' was developed. All it did was hold all the investments that exist in an index, in the proportion by which they contributed to the index. The return of an index fund is simply the return on the index, less costs.

This is a very cheap way of investing, because there is little research or trading cost involved in putting together a portfolio that has exactly the same investments as the index. As well as this, it immediately provides an extremely well diversified portfolio.

The portfolio theory that underpins the existence of index funds is known as the efficient market theory. It states that the forward expectations for a company's share price are so well priced into the current share price, that the current share price is the best estimate of the value of the company. This being the case, there is no point in spending time and money researching and trading trying to find mispriced investments.

It is worth keeping in mind that as an investor you don't have to come to a conclusion about whether index investing is superior to active management. Indeed, there is a trend towards using a combination of index funds and active funds in portfolios. The index funds provide a well diversified, low-cost 'core' to the portfolio, while the use of some active investing provides a 'satellite' effort to (hopefully) add investment performance over the index return.

Alpha and beta

'Alpha' and 'beta' have become the two investment terms used in the discussion of active and passive investment management. Beta refers to the overall market return. Alpha refers to the value added (or destroyed) above the average by active management. For example, if the average market return over a given period is 12 per cent, then the beta return, market return, is 12 per cent. A fund manager who achieved a return of 15 per cent — 3 per cent over the index — would refer to the 3 per cent outperformance as their alpha.

As an example of this terminology in practice, Q Super, the Queensland State Government superannuation fund that manages more than $20 billion in assets, announced an 'alpha-beta separation process' to manage its investment assets. The process involves Q Super adopting a 'core and satellite' approach to its portfolio, with the market return (beta) acknowledged as the primary source of investment returns, while still using active management to try and achieve returns above the market average (alpha).

Boutique fund managers

If the use of wraps is a strong trend in the financial services industry and worthy of comment, then another important trend is the rise of the boutique fund manager. Boutique fund managers are defined by a number of characteristics. They tend to be fund managers who:

- have built an investment reputation with a large fund manager and left to set up their own fund-management business
- operate much smaller managed funds than those of the big fund managers (such as AMP, Colonial First State and BT)
- often have their own money invested in the fund that they manage, and an ownership interest in the fund's management company
- usually have a specialist management focus, such as small company shares or international shares, with a defined investment style
- usually have an identifiable fund manager who runs the fund (such as Peter Morgan at 452 Capital or Peter Hall at Hunter Hall).

Often boutique fund managers start working at one of the large fund management companies, and then make a move to start their own operation. Examples of this include Paul Moore at PM Capital and Kerr Neilsen at Platinum, both of whom previously worked at BT. Peter Morgan left Perpetual Investments to set up 452 Capital and Anton Tagliaferro of Investors Mutual had previously worked at Perpetual Investments and BNP. This progression suggests the boutique managers are talented fund managers who want to move beyond the confines of the institutional fund management business and set up their own enterprise.

Earlier in this chapter we examined the difficulty that large managed funds have in effectively managing assets because of their size. The large amount of money that they are managing means they have difficulty in transacting efficiently in markets, and that the funds are forced to hold a large number of investments, simply because of their size. Boutique funds, with smaller amounts of money to manage, don't have this problem. They are far more able to invest meaningful portions of their managed fund in much smaller companies if they choose. A recent trend towards 'high conviction' managed funds, where fund managers build a concentrated portfolio of investments (of perhaps 15 to 30 investments), allows boutique fund managers to take a more aggressive approach to building a managed fund portfolio.

These managers are said to be 'index unaware' another relevant phrase which means they are not concerned with making the underlying portfolio look similar to the index. This criticism is levelled at many large managed funds.

Two Australian boutique fund management success stories are the Platinum International Fund and the Hunter Hall Value Growth Trust. Kerr Neilson runs the Platinum International Fund that, since inception in April 1995, has returned a compound annual return of 17.4 per cent a year. Peter Hall's record with the Hunter Hall Value Growth Trust is equally impressive, returning a compound annual return of 19.4 per cent since its inception in May 1994. (These statistics are the managed fund performance to 30 November 2006.)

Two drawbacks to boutique managed funds are that there is usually 'key person risk' tied to the main fund manager, and the boutique managed fund usually has quite a specific investment focus. Key person risk refers to the fact that if a boutique fund is led by a particularly talented manager, then the effect of their leaving the fund is likely to be significant. The specific investment focus of a managed fund, such as a focus on international small companies, means it is unlikely to be a 'one-stop' investment solution, and is better suited to being part of an overall portfolio.

Hedge funds

Hedge funds are an increasingly popular part of the investment landscape. Hedge funds, also referred to as absolute return funds, are managed funds in which the fund manager implements trading strategies to generate investment returns. These strategies can include borrowing money, trading derivatives, short selling (where the fund takes a position that benefits from falls in investment values), program trading and arbitrage trading (looking to trade on price differences of a stock or commodity listed on different exchanges). In short, hedge funds have a broad scope to act as a trading fund seeking investment returns.

The Reserve Bank of Australia (RBA), in a November 2006 bulletin entitled 'Recent Developments in the Australian Hedge Fund Industry', commented on the strong growth in hedge funds. The bulletin notes that the Australian hedge fund industry has grown much more quickly than either the broader managed fund industry in Australia or the global hedge fund industry. It says that in June 2000 the Australian hedge fund industry managed less than $2 billion and by June 2006 this had risen to $60 billion. About two-thirds of investors in Australian hedge funds are individuals, which is considerably higher than the global average.

Hedge funds are often promoted to investors as having a 'low correlation' to other asset classes, and the ability to 'make money from trading strategies in either rising or falling markets'. Low correlation to other asset classes means that the returns received from a hedge fund are not closely related to other asset classes. This is useful in an overall portfolio because hedge funds may provide a reasonable investment return at a time when other investment returns are poor, thus evening out the overall portfolio returns.

There remain good reasons to be cautious when considering hedge funds for an investment portfolio. The statistics clearly show they are a relatively new asset class in Australia, with only a short track record. With hedge funds being basically trading funds relying on the decisions of the fund manager to trade in high-risk investments such as derivatives, and with the use of borrowed money, the level of risk associated with this activity has to be acknowledged as high.

Most professional investment managers, such as institution superannuation fund managers, who use hedge funds use them as part of their 'alternative assets' within a portfolio, often making up less than 5 per cent of a portfolio. This would seem to be a prudent maximum allocation for an investor considering hedge funds for their portfolio.

Figures from the RBA bulletin show that about one-third of hedge fund investments are held in 'fund of fund' hedge funds. These are funds that comprise a number of different hedge investment managers and investment styles, in an effort to reduce the overall risk of the fund. This approach is worth considering for anyone contemplating a hedge fund investment.

Private equity

Private equity generally refers to investments in companies that are not publicly listed on a stock exchange. The nature of private equity has meant that it has, in the past, generally referred to smaller companies, in the stage before they list. However, as more and more money is available for private equity investment, there has been a trend toward private equity investors being able to purchase large public companies, or parts of companies, and running them privately. The aim of private equity funds is to make leveraged buyout (LBNO) takeovers, using a large amount of debt, and then to sell the company quickly — within three to five years — for a big profit, generally by listing or relisting it on the stock exchange.

There are a growing number of private equity managed funds available for investors. These managed funds often have high minimum investment balances and are relatively 'illiquid', that is, it may take a very long time for an investor to be able to sell their investment, if they can at all. As an example, Gresham Investment House is a private equity firm that has managed successful private equity funds for investors. In 2004 it established Gresham Private Equity Fund 2, which required a minimum investment of $50,000, although this amount was not all paid at the start of the investment, but in instalments as required. Since its establishment, the fund has made a number of purchases, including Pacific Print Group and Witchery Fashions. It is likely to be five or ten years before investors receive returns from their investment.

An alternative for investors to managed funds are private equity funds listed on the ASX. Because these funds are listed it is possible to buy and sell them more easily. The range of private equity listed investment companies includes Colonial Private Equity (stock code CFI), Macquarie Private Capital (MPG) and Souls Private Equity (SOE).

Private equity funds have a reputation for charging high investment fees. Therefore, it is important to understand the level of fees you are paying and to be comfortable with these fees before investing.

High-yield debentures and unsecured notes

Unsecured notes (similar to promissory notes) are issued by a finance company, usually for a set period, and offer investors an interest return for allowing the finance company the use of their money.

Debentures offer investors a similar income return for the use of their money, with investors ranking slightly higher on the list of a company's creditors if the company collapses.

High-yield debentures and unsecured notes are among some of the most heavily promoted investment options. At first glance they appear to offer a tremendous investment opportunity, providing:

- high investment returns (usually more than 3 per cent higher than the cash interest rate)
- strong, regular income payments
- no capital volatility.

Things are not as rosy as they seem, however. In February 2005, ASIC released a surveillance report into high-yield debentures. The report was not glowing, and included the following comments: 'We saw an increased use of debt offerings to retail investors to finance projects that, some years ago, would have been financed by the institutional or wholesale market' and 'We had disclosure concerns with many of the prospectuses.'

The report looked at nine high-yield debentures. During the course of the campaign stop orders were issued against Fincorp, Australian Capital Reserve, Hargraves Secured Investments and Victorian Finance and Leasing. The common issues related to prospectuses included:

- issues about disclosure of related-party transactions
- issues surrounding property valuation
- the capitalisation of interests on loans (which means rather than paying the interest when it falls due, companies were adding it to the loan and making interest payments to investors from new investors' money)
- bad or doubtful debts.

These are core issues for any investor looking to understand and assess the quality of the investment they plan to make in a debenture or unsecured notes.

If you are ever tempted to invest large portions of your portfolio into high-yield debentures or unsecured notes, keep the Westpoint collapse in mind. The investors in this scheme thought that they had found the perfect, high-yield, capital-secure investment scheme, but history shows that it was far riskier than people thought and the scheme collapsed.

Unsecured notes, promissory notes and debentures should always be treated with caution. The only reason any company offers investment returns of 9–14 per cent on borrowings is that it cannot find anyone prepared to lend it the money at a lower rate of interest. Keep in mind that if it is paying you a 9 per cent return, after fees and commissions, the loan is likely to be costing much more than this — and again, it is only paying this much because no one else will lend the money more cheaply. At the very least, read the February 2005 ASIC surveillance report before investing any money into this type of managed investment and, if you are still tempted, only do so with a small slice of your total investment capital.

Separately managed accounts

A recent addition to the investment landscape, separately managed accounts (also known as individually managed accounts), are another way investors can get access to professional investment management. Unlike managed funds, where money is pooled then invested on the fund's behalf, separately managed accounts keep each investor's money in their own account, with the investor having a portfolio directly managed on their behalf.

Two key benefits of this approach over managed funds is that investments can be specifically managed to meet your tax needs and, because there is less pooling of funds, it is much easier for a separately managed account to trade more efficiently than a managed fund.

Another big difference is that when you purchase a managed fund, you do so with an already established portfolio that may include unrealised capital gains. When the investments with these unrealised capital gains are sold, the managed fund investor will be liable for tax on the gains. A separately managed account means you are starting with your own portfolio, with no unrealised capital gains.

Clime Asset Management and Direct Portfolio are two Australian providers of separately managed accounts.

Managed fund researchers

A large part of the process of distributing managed funds by financial planners is the use of managed fund researchers to justify their recommendations. This process deserves further scrutiny.

It is worth starting with a paper written by Julia Sawicki, a finance academic, and Kevin Thomson, a financial planner, that examined two key inputs into the process of selection of managed funds: research company ratings and the past performance of managed funds. Their paper, 'An Investigation into the Performance of Recommended Funds: Do Managed Funds "Approved" by Research Companies Outperform the Non Gratea?' (which means not approved), studied two key approaches to choosing funds: the use of research companies to rate managed funds and the use of past performance to predict a fund that would outperform.

Sawicki and Thomson had access to the ratings from a research company for the six years from 1989 to 1995. They found no evidence that funds approved by the research company outperformed those that were non-approved. In fact, they set up two hypothetical portfolios in which $1000 was invested into each of the 14 categories of funds (capital stable, equity and international funds) and calculated the average returns for the approved funds and the non-approved funds. At the end of the six years the approved-fund portfolio was valued at $21,027 and the non-approved fund category was $21,540.

Their conclusion was clear: 'The results generally reveal no significant difference between the performance of approved and non-approved funds on a group as well as an individual basis, suggesting that the classic return-maximising investor would not be aided by the research companies' recommendations.'

The period that was studied was some time ago (1989–95) so it is worth looking at the present ratings system to see what value it may add to an investor. Possibly the best-known ratings company is Morningstar, which rates managed funds on a scale from one to five stars.

An article by Phillip Gray found on the Morningstar website provides some information on the methodology behind the star rating system. Funds are rated using a combination of three- and five-year returns data, with the results adjusted for the volatility of returns. A fund with a similar level of returns to another, but with greater volatility of returns, will receive a lower rating. Volatility is measured on the basis of monthly returns.

Funds are then allocated a star rating based on their historical return, adjusted for volatility. A five-star fund is in the best 10 per cent of funds of that type, a four-star fund the best 22.5 per cent, three stars the middle 35 per cent, two stars the next 22.5 per cent and a one star fund the worst 10 per cent.

This process of rating funds from one to five stars is completely quantitative, and does not capture the value that may be added by the qualitative process a researcher such as Morningstar will do. That said, the five-star system is a powerful and simple way of rating managed funds for investors. Clearly, this system is based heavily on historical returns, which was investigated in the second part of Sawicki and Thomson's study.

In looking at the ability of historical managed fund returns to predict future returns, Sawicki and Thomson found no evidence of 'persistence' of returns; that is, there was no evidence that choosing a managed fund that had outperformed in the past would provide above-average returns in the future.

This conclusion is one that has been reached by many researchers. Mark Carhart, in his famous paper 'On Persistence in Mutual Fund Performance' published in the *Journal of Finance* in 1997, found there was no evidence of persistence in the performance of managed funds. Academics Michael Drew and Jon Stanford of the University of Queensland, wrote a paper, 'Returns from Investing in Australian Equity Superannuation Funds, 1991–1999', published in the *Services Industry Journal* in 2003. They found 'no evidence that active fund management adds value' and 'the market for equities in Australia appears to be remarkably efficient'.

A more recent study by Matthew Morey from the Department of Finance at Pace University, New York, is titled 'The Kiss of Death: A 5 Star Morningstar Mutual Fund Rating?'. He examines equity funds from the 1990s that were granted a five-star Morningstar rating and finds that, 'there is a sharp drop-off in performance after a fund receives its first five-star Morningstar rating', which is 'very consistent with the literature that shows that a winning performance does not persist'.

The summary of this is simple: while a financial planner can tell with 100 per cent certainty the managed funds that have historically outperformed, research suggests that this is not of any great use when looking forward. This is why the warning 'that past performance is not an indicator of future performance' is so important: it just happens to be true.

Conclusion

It is easy to conclude from the information presented in this chapter that managed funds, the cornerstone of the structural corruption of the financial planning industry for a long time, are simply a bad investment option. This is not true. Indeed, it is likely that investors will have some use for managed funds at different times, if only to get access to asset classes that are difficult to access directly. Although managed funds are not a bad investment option themselves, they are also not the 'panacea for all' that sections of the financial planning industry suggest. There should always be a balance, and the best way to get that balance right for your portfolio is to be aware of the conflicts of interest surrounding managed funds, and to stay informed about their advantages and drawbacks.

Case study

Cheryl Basso couldn't believe her luck when she won a million dollars.

She decided to stick to her plan to retire in about five years and use the windfall to make her retirement that much sweeter. After hunting around for a financial adviser, Mr and Mrs Basso settled on a planner who seemed willing to meet their demands for no entry fees or commissions. The adviser devised a financial plan for an $800,000 investment. Half would be put into a managed fund, and $200,000 would be placed in each of their superannuation accounts. He recommended the funds be invested in an in-house managed fund.

The adviser told the Bassos in writing that the products would not involve upfront fees and he would receive brokerage payments which would cover the cost of his advice and work in preparing the investment proposal.

Three years later, Mr and Mrs Basso were unhappy with the arrangement and withdrew their funds. They claim they were charged undisclosed fees and commissions, and had not been told of investment options outside of the in-house products. Despite the fact there was clearly a commission being paid on the fund, it was explained away as 'paid by the fund manager at no cost to the client'. The Bassos in fact were being charged an extra 0.75 per cent over and above the standard management fees. As well, the adviser was receiving a $220 trailing commission each month.

The adviser explained that the documents he had prepared for the couple disclosed the fees and commissions in the 'fine print'. He denied bias led him to recommend the in-house fund. The adviser says he wasn't obliged to explain his assessment of other funds, but instead needed only to be sure there was a reasonable basis for the investment he recommended.

Mr and Mrs Basso took their claims to the Financial Industry Complaints Service, seeking $57,337 in compensation for poor financial planning and advice.

The complaints panel agreed the adviser failed to clearly inform them about alternative investment options: 'The panel is not satisfied that there has been adequate disclosure of fees and charges. Clients have the right to know what is the cost of doing business with an adviser.'

The financial adviser was ordered to pay $18,000 plus interest to Mr and Mrs Basso, as well as $3,840 compensation for not advising them of their right to receive a multiple product discount.

Chapter 8

SUPERANNUATION

For most of us, superannuation is or will be the largest investment we have apart from our home. It's also the largest investment we have as a nation. As at 30 June 2006, about ten million Australians had more than $913.9 billion invested in superannuation, which was up by 19.8 per cent on the previous year. This may seem like a lot of money, but when you consider that we currently have the highest life expectancy on record, it needs to be!

According to the Australian Bureau of Statistics, a baby boy born today can expect to live 78.5 years, while a baby girl can expect to live 83.3 years. Further, if we survive to age 65, men can expect to live another 18.1 years and women another 21.4 years.

The facts are that with longer life expectancy and an ageing population, most of us need to save more for retirement than we think, or than we are currently saving. To encourage us to do this, the government makes sure long-term money gets a tax break, making it one of the last legal tax dodges.

Rather than being taxed at your marginal rate, superannuation savings attract just 15 per cent tax on both contributions and fund earnings. Currently a 15 per cent tax rate also applies to benefit payments, but from 1 July 2007, superannuation benefits paid from a taxed fund as either a lump sum or allocated pension will be tax-free to anyone over 60.

Yet despite the size and tax-effectiveness of superannuation, many of us fail to give it the attention it deserves. For many of us, it seems too complex and retirement seems such a long way off (for some longer than others), but there is really no excuse for treating superannuation any differently to any other part of your life. You really need to see it as an integral part of your total wealth-creation strategy.

Furthermore, the federal budget 2006–07 made considerable inroads into making superannuation simpler (we will talk more about the announced changes later in this chapter), so it is more worthwhile than ever to review your superannuation and see how these changes may affect you.

In Australia, we have a unique three-pillared superannuation system that relies on three main sources of income: compulsory superannuation (known as the Super Guarantee), voluntary contributions and taxpayer-funded, means-tested pensions. It is the compulsory superannuation system component of our unique superannuation system (introduced in 1993 by Prime Minister Paul Keating) that can be credited for creating a truly buoyant superannuation industry in Australia and giving many of us a retirement benefit for our future.

But will it be enough? The answer depends on a few factors, including your age, how many years until you retire and your expectations of the type of retirement lifestyle you want. According to the Investment and Financial Services Association (IFSA), research conducted in 2005 by Rice Walker Actuaries found that Australians required a grand total of some $2641 billion to fund their retirement. Yet, based on savings and age pension levels, only $2189 billion was available, leaving a savings gap of $452 billion. Where will this money come from?

On an individual level, research conducted by Westpac for the Association of Superannuation Funds of Australia in September 2006 shed some light on just how much it could individually cost us to retire.

It found that a Sydney couple who owned their own home would need approximately $47,967 a year to have a comfortable retirement, which included eating out from time to-time, taking occasional overseas holidays and entertaining family and friends at home. A more modest retirement lifestyle could be sustained for $25,920 a year.

Most financial planners estimate investors should generally aim to save at least 60 or 65 per cent of their pre-retirement income to maintain the lifestyle they are accustomed to in retirement. This is more than the current Super Guarantee rate of 9 per cent provides, so the sad truth is that unless we take a more active approach to our superannuation, and do more than we have to, we will run short of money in our retirement. This is why the fees and charges that bleed our savings are so important. As we mentioned before, saving for retirement is a game of inches, in which small costs now add up to big costs when you retire.

The reality of not having enough money in retirement is having to draw on the age pension, the third pillar of the Australian superannuation system. But when you consider that singles receive approximately $13,300 a year and a couple receives $22,240 a year, this is not a comforting option.

Accessing your super

While superannuation money is definitely yours, access to it is structured so that while we are working we can't plunder it, so it continues to accumulate to maximise the end benefit.

In general, you can access your preserved benefits once you have retired after reaching your preservation age, are no longer working at 60 years and over, or you are aged 65.

Prior to this, all contributions and fund earnings from 1 July 1999 are preserved or unable to be drawn upon until you reach preservation age, which is dependent on when you were born.

That said, it is possible to access preserved superannuation benefits on compassionate grounds and severe financial hardship. Preservation age is currently being increased from 55 to 60 years, so that by 2025 it will be 60 years for anyone born after June 30, 1964.

The table below summarises the phase-in:

For a person born	Preservation age (years)
Before 1 July 1960	55
1 July 1960 – 30 June 1961	56
1 July 1961 – 30 June 1962	57
1 July 1962 – 30 June 1963	58
1 July 1963 – 30 June 1964	59
After 30 June 1964	60

Source: Australian Taxation Office

Any contributions or fund earnings before 1 July 1999 generally maintain their non-preserved status and fall into one of two categories.

- Restricted non-preserved benefits cannot be cashed until you satisfy a condition of release, such as terminating your employment in an employer superannuation scheme.
- Unrestricted non-preserved benefits do not require you to fulfil a condition of release and can be paid upon demand.

While these non-preserved funds can be accessed before retirement, investing them back into your superannuation fund makes a whole lot of sense because you could find you pay much more tax on these funds if you invest them outside of super.

Changes from July 2007

As mentioned in the introduction to this chapter, if you have not revisited the rules surrounding the treatment of superannuation money, it is worthwhile doing so because much is set to change from July 2007.

The proposed changes were announced as part of the federal budget delivered in May 2006, which outlined the government's plan to 'simplify and streamline' superannuation. The proposals are now contained in the Tax Laws Amendment (Simplified Superannuation) Bill 2006. There are a few gems in these proposals that few of us saw coming, including changes to the rules on cashing out super.

Although preservation laws are set to remain the same, the tax rules for cashing out your super will depend on your age, with the big winners being those aged over 60, who will now get to take out their super completely tax-free. Benefits paid from an untaxed fund will still be taxed, but if you are 60 or over the tax rate will be lower.

Age-based restrictions limiting tax-deductible super-annuation contributions will also be replaced with a streamlined set of rules. Further, the announcement to abolish the Reasonable Benefit Limit (or the maximum benefit you are permitted to receive on a concessionally taxed basis as either a lump sum or a pension) is another real win for all investors and will help us all plan for a better retirement.

Rules relating to pensions have also been simplified. A complying pension product purchased after September 2007 will no longer be 50 per cent assets test exempt and will therefore be treated in the same way as allocated pensions.

The pension asset test taper rate will be halved, from $3 to $1.50 per fortnight for every $1000 above the relative threshold. You will also be able to choose how much you draw down from your pension each year, based on your age.

Following is a brief summary of how the changes work for before and after-tax contributions.

Before-tax contributions

Under the proposals, your total concessional contributions will be limited to $50,000 a year, taxed at 15 per cent. This will include any money you contribute through salary sacrificing. (The $50,000 amount will be indexed, but will only increase once the indexed change is greater than $5000.)

If your total before-tax contributions exceed the limit, you will be taxed on the excess at the top marginal tax rate (plus Medicare levy).

If you're presently aged 50 or will turn 50 between 2007–08 and 2011–12, your concessional contributions will be limited to $100,000 a year. From the 2012–13 year, the maximum amount of contributions taxed at 15 per cent will return to the indexed $50,000 amount. (The $100,000 limit will not be indexed.)

After-tax contributions

At the moment, you may contribute to your super an unlimited amount of your own money after tax at any time, up to a certain age.

Under the proposals, your after-tax contributions will be limited to $150,000 a year. If your after-tax contributions exceed the limit, you will be taxed at the top marginal tax rate (plus Medicare levy).

For after-tax contributions made between 10 May 2006 and 30 June 2007, a transitional $1 million limit will apply.

If you're under age 65 and want to make a larger contribution, you will be allowed to bring forward two years of contributions. For example, you could contribute $450,000 in 2007–08 but will then be unable to make further after-tax contributions until the 2010–11 financial year. (Some exemptions apply for small-business owners and for people receiving settlements for an injury resulting in permanent disablement.)

All of these changes, amendments and simplifications provide a terrific opportunity to give your superannuation savings a boost and devise strategies to actively try and maximise your retirement benefit.

The best people to provide you with advice that is tailored to your needs and your retirement goals are licensed financial planners that are free from the conflicts of interest caused by sales commissions. We have compiled an up-to-date list of such planners to provide you with a starting point when seeking good advice. You'll find the list on The Eureka Way website (www.theeurekaway.com.au).

Superannuation vehicles

Superannuation would have to be the most tinkered-with legislation in the history of Australian politics and is has been subject to numerous tax changes, consultation processes and reviews. As a result, superannuation is a dynamic and ever-changing investment vehicle.

Probably the biggest change to be made to super, apart from the introduction of the Super Guarantee in 1993, has been the introduction of the choice of superannuation fund legislation on 1 July 2005, which has made most superannuation funds now open to the public.

Prior to this, most of us were directed by our employer to a superannuation vehicle of their choice. We simply ticked a box when we started a new job and that was that.

But now, under Super Choice the range of superannuation funds available is quite diverse and includes retail, corporate, industry and public sector funds, small APRA funds, retirement savings accounts and self-managed super funds.

The most common superannuation vehicle is retail funds, which at 30 June 2006, held 32.2 per cent of total assets.

This was closely followed by self-managed super funds with 23 per cent of total assets, industry funds with 16.9 per cent, public sector funds with 16.7 per cent and corporate funds with 5.9 per cent of total assets. Small APRA funds accounted for 0.3 per cent of total assets.

So what are the features of each of the fund types?

- *Retail funds*: These include commercially promoted public offer funds and master trusts. Wholesale arrangements can sometimes be negotiated by employers.
- *Corporate superannuation funds*: A superannuation fund established for the benefit of employees of a particular company or group of companies, or group of employers.
- *Industry superannuation funds*: These are multi-employer superannuation funds. An industry fund may cover a specific industry or a range of industries, either nationally or within a state. Some industry funds are public-offer funds.
- *Public sector superannuation funds*: These are superannuation funds that provide benefits for federal, state, territory or local government employees.
- *Small APRA funds*: This is a superannuation fund with four or fewer members that is administered by an approved trustee and which is not a public-offer fund. They are regulated by the Australian Prudential Regulation Authority (APRA).
- *Retirement savings accounts*: Accounts offered by banks, building societies, credit unions, life insurance companies and prescribed financial institutions. It is used for retirement savings and is capital-guaranteed.
- *Self-managed super funds*: A superannuation fund of four or fewer members, in which all members are trustees of the fund. If the trustees are individuals, all trustees are members of the fund, or if the trustee is a company all members are directors of the company and all directors are members of the fund. There is a further requirement that no member can be an employee of another member of the fund unless the members

involved are related. Special rules apply for single-member funds and when members are co-directors of a company. Self-managed superannuation funds are supervised by the Australian Taxation Office.

Irrespective of which superannuation vehicle you use, you need to be aware of how much it costs you per year to invest with a particular fund. Also, what other benefits are provided by your fund? What are the insurance levels? Is there access to financial planning services? What has been the performance of the fund over a five-year period?

You can change superannuation funds at any time, but you are only able to change funds once a year. If you are eligible to choose superannuation funds, you can get a standard choice form from your employer.

Under choice of superannuation fund legislation, you are eligible to choose the fund for your future superannuation guarantee contributions unless:

- your super is paid under a state award or industrial agreement
- your super is paid under a certified agreement or an Australian Workplace Agreement
- you're a federal or state public sector employee excluded from choice by law or regulations
- you're in a particular type of 'defined benefit' fund or you've already reached a certain level of benefit in that fund. (A defined benefit fund is a superannuation fund where a formula for calculating the retirement benefit is based on terms of service with the employer and average salary level over the few years prior to retirement.)

Investment choice

On top of fund choice, you also have investment choice — the power to decide what investment funds you would like to invest your money in to help grow your super. Within superannuation vehicles there is an array of investment funds designed to help you maximise your retirement savings. They cover the main asset classes — Australian and international shares, fixed interest, property and cash — but can also include ethical and socially responsible investing options. You can make your own fund choices or you may be able to choose an investment plan within a superannuation fund.

Investment plans offer you a ready-made group of funds based on your risk profile and return expectations. In some ways they can narrow down the field and give you a guide to investing if you're really not sure where to start.

Either way, the key to selecting the right investment choice is to understand both your risk profile and your investment horizon. To do this, you should know your own attitudes to risk and return. That is, are you willing to take on more risk to try and eke out a slightly higher return, or will this approach just make you anxious? So it's that old risk/return trade-off and it's really about your comfort levels.

Your investment horizon is how long you plan to invest your money. While it might be rightly assumed that for most people, superannuation is a long-term investment, if you are approaching retirement age you may want to focus on preserving your capital and employ a capital-protection strategy that invests in defensive assets such as fixed interest and cash.

Alternatively, if you are just starting your working life and contributing to superannuation, it makes sense to employ a more aggressive investment strategy. The argument here is that you have a longer time frame to ride out the inherent volatility in investment markets, so investing in asset classes such as shares and property may enable you to grow your savings more aggressively.

Switching superannuation funds

There are several reasons why you may decide to switch superannuation funds, such as starting a new job, looking to consolidate your superannuation or if you are dissatisfied with your existing superannuation fund and want to find an alternative. However, you may find that while you did not choose your current superannuation fund yourself, it could actually be the most cost-effective fund for you and the one that is best suited to your needs.

To make this decision you need to understand how and why an alternative superannuation fund would be better than your current fund. To do this you need to look at fees, investment performance, insurance coverage and any other services the fund offers.

There may also be some hidden features of your current fund. For example, your employer may contribute more to your superannuation fund than the compulsory 9 per cent, so you should find out from your employer whether there are other benefits around your superannuation that are related to how long you stay with the company or, indeed, if your money only becomes yours after you have been with the company for a certain period of time.

Performance is a crucial factor in comparing super-annuation funds and one that is affected by not only the performance of investment markets, but also by the fee structure of a fund.

The most important thing to compare when looking at a fund's performance is its investment results over the long term, because superannuation is a long-term investment and you are not looking to change your superannuation fund every week. Certainly, you should take any promises with a pinch of salt.

It is best to look at a superannuation fund's average returns over a five- to ten-year period. By doing this, you can smooth out any bumps in the shorter-term performance results, which may exaggerate the very good or very poor performance of a particular fund.

Second, you need to compare like with like. If you are looking at the performance of your growth-style investment — that is, one that is more heavily weighed towards shares and property — compare it with other growth-style investment options.

Also, remember what we mentioned earlier: the impact that fees can have on your fund's performance results, especially over the long-term, tend to magnify the actual drain effect fees can have on your final payout. ASIC estimates that if you pay an extra 1 per cent each year in fees over a 30-year period, you could reduce your final retirement benefit by up to 20 per cent. This is a scary prospect, but one worth knowing while you can still do something about it.

And be especially careful when a financial planner who may be receiving a commission recommends that you switch funds. ASIC surveys have found that this is often poor advice, motivated by the adviser's desire to make a buck — not by what is in your best interests (see details below).

Fees have been a central plank in the marketing campaigns of many superannuation funds since the introduction of super choice, particularly industry superannuation funds, which argue they not only have lower average fees, but also do not pay commissions to financial planners. They say this means they can focus on delivering better returns to their members.

This claim has been supported by some research. SuperRatings, an independent rating business, has conducted research on behalf of industry super funds to demonstrate that the net benefit to members over the past one, three and five years was higher in an industry fund than in a retail master trust vehicle. For more information on the results of this research, visit www.industryfunds.org.au/researchsays.

Insurance

Another important area of comparison between super-annuation vehicles is insurance coverage. It is important not to assume that coverage is standard within all superannuation funds. In some cases it will be compulsory, but in other funds you may have to qualify. Further, age restrictions may apply.

While medical examinations may not be compulsory, automatic cover is not necessarily a good thing if it is not enough cover. Insurance coverage offered by superannuation funds commonly extends to life and disability cover, but does not include other forms of insurance, such as income protection.

Research released by ChantWest Financial Services for IFSA in May 2005 demonstrated that there can also be huge variations in premiums across superannuation funds. It found that someone could pay 22 times more for the same cover at another superannuation fund.

Insurance premiums can have a significant impact on your retirement age and final benefit, so it is not only important to get comprehensive cover, but also cost-effective insurance cover.

So why is there a price differential between premiums? Different types of superannuation funds take into consideration different factors when pricing their premiums. For example, the ChantWest research found that industry funds generally base the level of cover and premiums on age only, so there is a high degree of cross-subsidisation within these funds.

ASIC's consumer website has a great tool for testing 'what ifs' when it comes to the long-term effects of various factors; it's a very useful tool when assessing and comparing your superannuation fund. These factors include:

- the most common fees charged by various funds
- making extra contributions

- receiving government co-contributions, if you are eligible
- breaking or reducing contributions as a result of time out of the workforce
- switching your investment strategy or changing funds.

To use the tool, go to www.fido.asic.gov.au. For more information on the choice of superannuation fund legislation, visit www.superchoice.gov.au.

If after a process of collecting information on your current fund and other fund options, you are serious about switching superannuation funds, it is a good idea to get some good financial advice. This is because a financial planner can assess your individual circumstances and can tailor their advice to your needs.

This tip may seem a bit strange, even dangerous, considering the shocking results of a recent high-profile surveillance campaign conducted by ASIC on the advice financial planners were giving their clients following the introduction of super choice. First let's look at the results of the survey.

Conducted between June and December 2005, the survey assessed 306 examples of advice given to consumers and found that based on the client's needs, 16 per cent of advice was regarded as 'not reasonable' and a further 3 per cent was 'probably not reasonable'. Where consumers were advised to switch funds, one third of this advice lacked 'credible reasons and risked leaving the consumer worse off'.

Alarmingly, the provision of unreasonable advice was three to six times more common if the adviser had an actual conflict of interest over the advice given to the client. These conflicts included such things as higher remuneration or product ties with the adviser's licensee. Meanwhile, ASIC has conducted follow-up action with 14 licensees and super giant AMP Financial Planning has been issued with an

Enforceable Undertaking — a legally binding commitment to lift its game and modify the way it provides financial advice to investors.

Given this research, why get advice about switching super at all? Well, on a positive note, the strategic advice provided in the survey around issues such as asset allocation, how much to contribute to super and tax advantages, were regarded as generally helpful to consumers.

The truth is that regulation within the financial planning industry has been greatly strengthened over the past three years, so the industry is in a major state of transition from one that was focused on selling product to one that is now more focused on providing good advice. As long as you know a bit about how the industry works, what to be aware of and how to protect yourself from getting 'bad' advice — and reading this book represents a good start — getting good independent advice does make sense.

Elsewhere in this book we explain how to get the best out of the financial planning industry. You can also check out The Eureka Way website at www.theeurekaway.com.au for a list of fee-for-service financial planners.

Consolidating super

It is not uncommon to have several superannuation accounts. Unless you stayed in the same job or industry all your life, you were probably asked by each new employer to join the superannuation fund that they used.

As a result, according to *Choice* magazine, there are 2.8 superannuation accounts for every Australian worker and research has shown that under the current superannuation arrangements, having multiple accounts can reduce your final benefit by 25 per cent. This is because every superannuation fund in your name is charging management and administration fees, all of which are eating into your retirement savings.

Based on this, there is a very strong argument for consolidating your super, not only so you can keep track of it, but to also reduce the fees you are paying. However, superannuation funds can charge exit fees when you close your account with them, so you need to work out whether it is worth paying these fees to consolidate your superannuation.

It's generally the older-style superannuation accounts, bought from life insurance companies in the 1980s and 1990s, that charge exit fees. Here the exit fee often doesn't expire until you reach a certain age or a particular account balance. It could cost a member about $1700 to withdraw from such a fund.

In some circumstances, you might feel it is prudent to have a few super accounts. This could be the case if you're looking to have a superannuation fund outside the one your employer may contribute to or if, for diversification purposes, you feel it is better to spread your super across different vehicles. Either way, both strategies have merit as long as the benefits to you outweigh the costs.

If you are interested in consolidating your super, visit the Australian Taxation Office website at www.ato.gov.au. It runs a number of services to help you track down your 'lost' super, including a lost members register and SuperSeeker, a tool designed to track down your super in real time.

Ways of topping up your super

Irrespective of your superannuation vehicle, there are several strategies you can employ to maximise your superannuation benefits. For example, for people who earn less than $28,000 a year, the federal government is currently offering a co-contribution scheme whereby it pays $1.50 for on every additional dollar you contribute to your own superannuation (up to a maximum of $1500).

The co-contribution scheme is available for people earning between $28,000 and $58,000 a year. It is adjusted depending on your income and how much you voluntarily contribute to your super fund. This scheme is available to low-income earners making less than $28,000 and tapers off as income increases up to $58,000. Some conditions do apply so it is worth familiarising yourself with the options. For more information visit www.asfa.asn.au.

Probably the simplest and most common way to contribute to your super is through salary sacrificing. This effectively gives your employer the authority to pay some pre-tax funds from your salary directly to your super fund over and above the compulsory superannuation rate.

As the funds are coming out of your salary before you pay tax, you end up paying less income tax, and because you don't see the funds first, you are not relying on your own discipline to invest the funds when you remember.

In some households, a spouse may earn very little super so it can be a tax-effective strategy to make spouse contributions and reduce the total tax bill for the family. There are limits set on how much can be contributed in a spouse's name. If your spouse earns less than $10,800 a year, you can also make an undeducted or after-tax contribution of $3000 to their super account. This strategy will earn you a tax rebate of $540, one that you can claim every year.

Chapter 9

DOING IT YOURSELF

After reading the earlier chapters in this book, about the problems of getting decent advice and the structure of the funds management industry, you're probably a bit curious about the alternatives. Here's the main one: Do It Yourself.

But taking the step from curious to serious and then to actually doing it is a big one and if you decide to take that leap, you will be putting yourself well and truly in the driving seat of your financial future. Any mistakes will be yours alone, along with the consequences. Then again, you will be in control — and you can always buy the bits of expertise you need, instead of putting your affairs entirely in someone else's hands.

For many investors, this is exactly how it should be. After all, don't we all manage family budgets, plan our finances for future expenses, manage debt and actively save for our retirement? Based on this argument, DIY investing is just an extension of our existing financial responsibilities.

And although there is some truth in this, to do DIY investing successfully, you really need to ramp up your expectations on just how involved you will be and the level of responsibility you will need to have.

This is particularly so with DIY super, where failure to establish and manage a self-managed superannuation fund (SMSF) correctly has serious legal consequences, including civil and criminal action with a maximum penalty of $220,000 and/or five years' jail.

The regulator of the SMSF industry, the Australian Taxation Office (ATO), also has the power to make an SMSF non-complying. This means the fund loses its beneficial tax treatment and may be taxed at 47 per cent instead of the concessional superannuation tax rate of 15 per cent. So DIY investing is a serious business and should be treated with due caution.

Scare tactics aside, DIY investing is a very doable investment option, one that a well-informed individual with a sound and tax-sensitive investment strategy can use to build and protect their wealth.

Benefits of DIY investing

The main benefit of DIY investing is of course the opportunity to take greater control of your financial future and pay less in fees. *You* decide the structure of your investments, the investment vehicles and products to be used and how you will keep track of your investments, and you don't just hand your savings over to someone who might be extracting fees and commission that erode your wealth.

The benefits of DIY investing are applicable to both superannuation and any investments outside of super. So in the case of superannuation, an SMSF allows you to create an investment portfolio that matches your specific needs. For example, perhaps you have many years to retirement and want to take quite an aggressive approach and invest mainly in growth assets such as equities and property. The investment plan can be structured to deliver this.

Alternatively, you may only have a few years to retirement and want to focus on protecting your accumulated wealth in the most tax-effective manner. An SMSF can do this too.

Although both features are available in other investment and superannuation vehicles, the full benefit can be reduced due to the pooling characteristic of investment products such as large super funds and managed fund products, which tend to be one-size-fits-all and where you also can inherit the fund's tax liability.

In an SMSF you get to choose when assets are bought and sold, giving you more control over capital gains. In some circumstances, SMSFs can be used specifically as a tool to minimise tax. For example, it may be possible to house your share portfolio within the fund, making the most of superannuation's beneficial tax treatment. This sounds fabulous, but it also means you will not be able to access your money until retirement.

Wealth creation, DIY-style

Warren Buffett, known as the world's greatest investor, had two basic investment rules:

- Don't lose money.
- Don't forget about rule number one.

That's a bit simplistic, but wealth creation really is as much about protecting your assets as it is about building them. So it's important to balance your growth strategies with some insurance designed to preserve your wealth.

To extend Mr Buffett's rules, here are ten more that can be applied when approaching DIY investing.

Rule1: Investing is all about the risk–return trade off

This is the inescapable bedrock of investing: the greater the return, the greater the risk. Investors caught up in the Westpoint collapse were getting 12 per cent 'guaranteed' yield, but they either forgot the risk–reward principle or didn't know it. With the interest rate on government bonds at a little more than 5 per cent there is no such thing as a guaranteed 12 per cent yield or even a safe 12 per cent yield.

In effect, the basic purpose of investing your money is to be paid for taking risk with it, and the more your risk you take, the more you should be paid. The regulator of the Australian financial services industry, Australian Securities & Investments Commission (ASIC), estimates that at least 6000 Australians have lost about $500 million of their savings chasing high returns.

What are high returns? Any investment that advertises it can deliver a return that is 2 per cent above that of similar established products is considered high. The common rule of thumb is that if an investment seems too good to be true, it most likely is.

Rule 2: Use the power of compounding

Albert Einstein is reputed to have said that compound interest is the most powerful force in the universe. Maybe he did, maybe he didn't say this, but it's still a powerful statement. In effect, all saving is an attempt to harness that power. If you reinvest your dividends and income, you will earn interest on your interest and, over time, your investment will grow in size rapidly.

For example, $10,000 invested at 7 per cent a year compounded becomes $38,697 after 20 years and $149,745 after 40 years. And if you invest just $50 a week at a return of 7 per cent during your working life of 40 years, you will end up with $534,024, thanks to the power of compounding.

Apart from additional contributions and the reinvesting of income, another great way to make the most out of compounding is with your tax refund. Even though your refund may be small, the power of compounding means that even small additional payments over time can make a big difference by either reducing the amount of interest you are paying on your debt or increasing the interest you are earning on your investments.

Rule 3: Diversify to reduce risk

This is usually expressed as 'don't put all your eggs in one basket'; it's a pretty common and well-understood principle.

Conversely, the most common mistake with diversification is to diversify too much. It simply isn't true that the more things you invest in, the less risk you are taking, so you don't need to have hundreds of investments: ten or 20 will usually do.

You can diversify across asset classes — say, shares or property — as well as within asset classes. Given that riskier assets derive greater returns, to help manage risk, it is best to spread the risk over a range of asset classes such as property, fixed interest, shares and cash.

By diversifying within a certain asset class it means that in a portfolio of ten resource stocks there will be considerably less risk than if all the money was invested in a single stock.

Another main benefit of diversifying arises from the lack of correlation between performing asset classes. This means that when one asset class or sub-category is performing well, another may not. If your portfolio is diversified across asset classes, poor performance by the riskier assets will not sink your life savings; some of your capital will still be protected by safer asset classes.

Rule 4: Choose investments you are comfortable with and which meet your needs. When in doubt, get advice

Investment products are designed by people who are looking to sell these products and they will not automatically be suitable for every investor. This is why it is essential that you take the time to consider your personal and financial goals *before* you invest.

Capital growth is derived when a capital gain is made — that is, when an investment is sold for more than you paid for it. It is most commonly associated with shares, which are regarded as a riskier and long-term investment.

Income-generating investments, such as cash and fixed-interest investments provide investors with an income over the term of their investment, providing a natural balance to the growth assets.

Knowing your goals will help define your time horizon (for how long you plan to invest the money). They will also help decide what asset classes are most suitable. For example, if you are investing for the short-term you will probably look at the cash and fixed-interest asset classes, while a long-term investment would be more suited for investing in Australian and international shares and property.

Rule 5: Don't forget tax

The most significant hidden cost for investors is not management fees, but tax. The reason for this is that fund managers usually don't think about the capital gains tax implications of what they do.

Often they do not hold stock for a 12-month period, thereby incurring capital gains tax on the whole investment, which is largely because they are investing on behalf of wide range of people with different time horizons and tax arrangements. If they hold a stock for longer than 12 months, they only pay tax on half the proceeds. In the case of super, the tax rate falls to 10 per cent.

These days the most important way to invest for the best tax-effective returns is via direct share investment and equity trusts, which can pay franked dividends. This means that a yield of 7 per cent is effectively equivalent to a 10 per cent return from a fixed-interest security. Also, in the case of property trusts, they often pay a high proportion of their annual unit-holder return as tax-exempt or tax-deferred income.

Then of course there is superannuation, the most tax-effective investment of all.

Rule 6: Invest in what you understand

It's a good idea to start close to home when you invest. Do you know and respect the company you work for? What about the places you shop or the car you drive? Have you had really good service from a company?

It's the little things that often tell you a company is well run, and good management always starts at the top. If you haven't had personal dealings with a company you are going to invest in, do some research.

You don't have to try and be an expert about everything, but it's your money and if you choose to invest, you are going to have to live with the consequences of your decision. You are probably going to give your money to someone else to manage — whether you invest directly in a company through a fund manager — so make sure you know all about them and understand how they invest.

All licensed financial institutions produce a Financial Services Guide (FSG), which provides information on the services and products offered as well as the remuneration structure. It is important to read this information before you buy a financial product or receive financial advice from them.

Another important document is a Product Disclosure Statement (PDS). This must be provided when you are recommended managed investments, superannuation products, insurance products, retirement savings accounts, deposit products and derivatives.

A PDS explains the features of a product, fees, the benefits and risks of investing, commissions that may affect your returns, information about complaints handling and cooling-off rights, and other information that may impact your decision to invest.

Companies produce prospectuses and annual reports. Yes, they often either look complex and hard to understand or simply like glossy brochures designed to sell you something, but they also contain prescribed information designed to help you understand the investment, so they are always worth the effort.

Rule 7: It's the people in a business that matter

This goes for listed companies and financial intermediaries. It is easy to get distracted by the large names and brands in the financial services industry, yet these do not tell you anything about the people actually doing the grunt work — the brains, if you like, behind the business. While it is hard for small investors to get to know corporate managers in the way large investors can, you can generally get a pretty good idea what they are like.

The big question for many investors is, does top performance come from the people managing the fund or the corporate structure behind the fund? It's probably a combination of both factors. However, the only way to investigate this question is to ask questions, scour websites, read information brochures and find out about the track record of the people behind the performing funds. The same goes for companies.

Make sure there hasn't been any significant loss of investment personnel before investing in a managed fund. Key-man risk plagues many top-performing funds and companies; you'd like to think that the success of a company or investment that you invest in does not ride on the back of one person.

Rule 8: Remember the importance of long-term trends

History is not the best guide to future performance, but it's the only one we've got. In this way, we can use it as a guide in selecting our investments and managing our return expectations.

It is also important to look for long-term quality in a fund's performance, which suggests an ability to deal with the inevitable ups and downs of markets.

So rather than just focusing on a fund or a company's stellar performance over the past 12 months, look beyond this. Look at its performance over periods such as five and seven years, periods in which the fund may have experienced a change in market conditions and had to adapt.

Also, watch the peaks and troughs of investment cycles. It is this historical perspective that best demonstrates how the market reverts to long-term trends and perhaps may help you sleep at night when your investments are going through a trough.

Rule 9: Building wealth is about time in the market, not timing the market

Building wealth requires a disciplined approach to investing, where you remain invested and you don't jump in and out of the market trying to time its ups and downs, paying costs every time you do. Remember, time out of the market can be costly too.

It's also true that there are times when you should not buy shares, because they are overpriced and are likely to fall. It took 25 years for the Dow Jones index in the United States to get back to where it was in September 1929; those who invested in the Nasdaq in early 2000 are still waiting for their investments to rise back to half the index's value at the time.

Discipline can be difficult to stick to when your investments are experiencing some volatility and you feel you might be losing your nerve. This is why it is important to have a strategy in place at the outset, including some diversification, so that if some of your investments do take a downturn you have another part of your portfolio giving you some stability.

In addition, by maintaining a consistent investment approach, sticking to your strategy and making additional contributions to your investments over time, you can also make the most of dollar-cost averaging.

Rule 10: Asset allocation is king

It is widely acknowledged that the mix of asset classes you have in your investment portfolio will have the greatest impact on the performance of your investments. Some investment gurus believe asset allocation is everything.

Their opinion aside, spreading your investments across a range of asset classes such as property, international and Australian shares, fixed interest and cash can make good sense for diversification benefits. It also gives you exposure to both growth and income assets that will perform well at different times and help you ride the wave of fluctuating returns.

This is because of the historically low correlation between the performance of growth assets such as international and Australian shares and defensive assets such as fixed interest.

By investing across asset classes, you can better manage the volatility inherent in most investment portfolios. This means a smoother ride for your investments and will no doubt allow you to sleep better at night.

Asset allocation is highly personal and will depend on your investment goals and time horizon, your risk tolerance and your financial situation, which will change as your circumstances change. So while you will need to dig deep when your portfolio rides the wave of market fluctuations, you also need to know when it is time to change your goals and realign your investment strategy with your new circumstances.

Making the DIY decision

The decision about whether to go DIY comes down to the time you have to dedicate to investing, your tolerance for taking risk, your skill level and most importantly, your level of common sense. That is the most important attribute for a DIY investor. You should ask the following questions before setting up an SMSF:

- Is the fund being established purely to manage your retirement benefits? If there is any other motive, your fund will not comply with existing regulations and you will be penalised.
- Do you have the necessary time and skills to manage your own super? It will be your responsibility to ensure the fund is set up correctly, that records are kept, reporting requirements are met, an appropriate investment strategy is set in line with the objectives of the fund and, most importantly, that the fund prospers in a way that justifies the cost and effort. Otherwise why bother?
- Are the benefits worth the costs? It is estimated an SMSF can cost approximately $1700 a year to manage. Due to this cost, it is estimated that it needs an initial investment of at least $200,000 to make it viable.
- What does the SMSF structure offer you that your existing super vehicle does not? Answering this question could require some professional advice. A financial planner can evaluate your personal circumstances and weigh up the benefits of an SMSF in comparison to your existing or other superannuation vehicles. An accountant can help you with establishing a SMSF but they cannot provide you with a comparison to other vehicles or offer investment advice unless they are licensed to do so.

These questions are just as relevant to your investments outside of superannuation and a financial planner can help you make the decision whether or not an SMSF is a good idea.

Making a financial plan, DIY-style

Financial planning has raised its head a few times already in the discussion of DIY investing due to its invaluable role in setting an investment course and giving some structure and strategy to your investing. But the difficulty can be in finding independent, value-for-money financial advice, free of the conflicts of interest inherent in the funds management industry.

You might be interested in using one of the financial planning software packages now available. These are designed to assist DIY investors with the preparation of a financial plan. They work in a similar way to the real-life financial planning experience in that they use your personal and financial information to develop your risk profile.

Using information such as your age, income, assets, desired retirement age and retirement income savings, the program will calculate not only what you need to save to achieve your desired retirement lifestyle, but an investment strategy that can help you achieve this.

Any investment strategy requires a risk/reward trade-off, and while a software program can recommend an asset allocation that can achieve your desired income level, it is totally dependent on the static information you supply. Unlike a financial planner, a computer program can obviously not ask probing questions designed to dig deeper into your attitudes to risk, a central element when designing an appropriate investment strategy.

That said, these tools have their place. As do the calculators available at the ASIC consumer website, FIDO, which has a number of useful tools to help you become more informed about who you are as an investor and the potential impact of your investment decisions. This website has tools ranging from a superannuation calculator, which will work out what your superannuation will be worth in the future, to a budget planner and a risk and return tool that allows you to see the impact different asset allocations have on returns. To use these tools, go to www.fido.asic.gov.au. You can also look at www.theeurekaway.com.au; we also have a range of tools and information for DIY investors.

Cost-effective investing

Discount fund brokers, wholesale funds and index funds are alternative investment options that can be both cost- and tax-effective for the DIY investor.

Discount fund brokers

Discount brokers are a growing force in the Australian market because they allow investors to access mainstream funds without the fees. So while no financial advice is provided on the suitability of particular funds, a discount broker is able to rebate 100 per cent of the entry fees on initial investment and contributions to many of the best-known fund manager products.

Some discount brokers even offer a portfolio management service and the ability to monitor your managed funds online. Discount fund brokers we know of include Commonwealth Securities, Direct Access, TD Waterhouse, E*Trade, Your Prosperity, InvestSMART and Neville Ward Direct.

Wholesale funds

Accessing wholesale funds is another way of avoiding some of the high entry fees on investment products. The Australian investment market is broken up into wholesale and retail markets. The wholesale market is generally made up of larger institutions and super funds, while the retail market is made up of individual investors.

Wholesale funds and retail funds invest in the same underlying funds but they have different price structures. In essence, wholesale funds have higher investment minimums (starting at about $50,000) and lower management expense ratios (MERs), ranging from 0.5–1 per cent a year. Historically, the boundaries between the two markets were quite defined, but the emergence of platform products such as master trusts and wrap accounts have broken down these distinctions.

Master trusts and wrap accounts give retail investors access to a range of wholesale managed funds, providing consolidated reporting on all their investments. While accessing wholesale funds should in theory reduce the overall costs to the investor, platform products have created a whole new layer of fees, including administration costs.

Industry super funds

Since the inception of choice of superannuation fund legislation in July 2005, industry superannuation funds have really come into the fore, with high-profile advertising campaigns and a willingness to challenge the dominance of retail master trusts.

Industry superannuation funds provide a cost-effective alternative to other commercial retail investment products that charge higher management fees and pay commissions to financial planners.

Industry funds advocate an administration fee of $1 or so a week, as well as a strong investment return track record. Both these factors are crucial in building your retirement savings over the long term. For more information visit www.industrysuper.com.

Index funds

Last on our list of alternative investments is index funds, a DIY investor's friend when it comes to a market rate of return with low costs and no hidden tax bill.

Index funds are a type of managed fund with a unique management style: unlike most managed funds that are actively managed through the buying and selling of assets, index funds are passively managed. That is, index managers construct an investment portfolio that closely matches a benchmark index, such as the All-Ordinaries index. They hold stocks longer than active fund managers, creating fewer transaction costs.

Given this style of management, they do not have the management costs of actively managed funds. One of the largest index fund managers in Australia is Vanguard Investments.

Keeping track of your investments

Administering and managing your investments is of central importance in any successful DIY investment strategy. Platform products or administration vehicles are the most common way investors manage their money.

Platform products

Platform products are promoted by financial planners as the best tool around. This approach suits financial planners because platform products were in fact designed by product manufacturers to help planners manage multiple client accounts. They provide a single entry point to a client's portfolio, making it easier for tax reporting and reviews.

The most important issue to be aware of with platforms is their fees. Platform products often have a bundled fee structure that includes a fund manager fee (or MER), an adviser fee and a platform administration fee. You pay all of these extra fees when you could have paid one fee and invested directly in a retail fund.

The argument is that despite this layering of fees, investors are still ahead because they get to invest at a wholesale rate and therefore pay lower up-front fees. This is not always the case. (See the chapter on platforms for more information.)

As a guide, the average MER for a platform — including all fees and commissions — is approximately 2 per cent a year and can be as high as 4 per cent. There are more than 40 platform providers to choose from, so scrutinise their fees before you make a choice.

Given that investing directly in a managed fund could cost you about 2 per cent, you really need to weigh up the benefits of a platform in providing consolidated reporting, access to wholesale funds you might not be able to access as a retail investor and tax reporting.

But in some circumstances platform products can be useful to the DIY investor. This may be the case if you have a number of individual investments and are looking for a way to streamline the management and paperwork associated with these investments. This is a particularly useful feature at tax time, as platform products provide consolidated tax reporting.

Administration services

There are other alternatives to using a platform product. For example, many accountants monitor and administer their clients' investments on their behalf. Such involvement can be a beneficial service for investors, as accountants obviously have a professional understanding of the tax implications embedded in existing assets and income streams. They can also conduct the appropriate annual reporting. But it can be an expensive way to administer your investments, because many accountants charge by the hour.

Unless they are licensed to do so, accountants are not allowed to provide financial advice. Some accountants have informal business alliances with financial advisers, and may be able to refer you to a financial planner. This approach can work well because it usually means your accountant and financial planner can take a collaborative approach to your finances and bring together the best of both worlds: tax information and investment strategy.

Because DIY investing is such a huge growth area in this country, there has been an explosion in the type and variety of products designed to assist DIY investors in managing and administering their portfolios.

To give you a feel for the range and type of administration services now on offer in the market, we have put together a list of providers we know of. This list is by no means definitive.

- *Praemium Portfolio Services* offers a sophisticated online share portfolio management tool only available through accountants, stockbrokers, superannuation administrators and financial planners.

    Praemium is really a service that has been designed around the recording and managing of capital gains tax consequences. It is a flat-fee service that is only available on a wholesale basis through accountants, financial planners and the retail services listed below. The level of sophistication really depends on the level of service your financial planner or accountant provides. For more information visit www.praemium.biz.
- *My PA Services* is a accountancy business that specialises in personal financial administration. It uses Praemium for its administrative platform. For a fixed fee, My PA Services offers a suite of personal administration services designed for DIY investors, for the financial services industry as well as access to online DIY portfolio administration software. For more information, see www.mypa.com.au.

- *Financial Shoebox* also uses Praemium for its administrative platform and offers web-based access to all your financial information to provide DIY with investors automatic record keeping, CGT optimisation, daily share price valuations and performance comparisons.

    Financial Shoebox operates on a flat-fee structure. They charge, on average, a $240 set-up fee, a $19 monthly access fee and an administration and maintenance cost ranging from $49 to $99, depending on whether you are passive, active or a trader. For more information see www.shoebox.net.au.

- *TrailCap* is an administration service that collects all the trailing commissions you pay on your managed funds, super and allocated pension investments and rebates any money collected over a $396 annual threshold. For more information visit www.investsmart.com.au.

- *SmartSuper* focuses on the administration of super, particularly self-managed super funds with more than $300,000, offering assistance with investment strategy preparation, regular reporting on investment values and performance, preparation of accounts and fund audits. For more information visit www.SmartSuper.com.au.

- *Cavendish Superannuation* specialises in the establishment and ongoing administration of self-managed superannuation.

    The establishment of a new fund will set you back $895, while compliance administration of an accumulation fund costs $1440 a year and $1680 for a pension fund. For more information visit www.cavendishsuper.com.au.

- *Super Concepts* is the self-managed fund specialist arm of ING. It can provide as much or as little support you want in managing your own superannuation fund.

Services range from help with setting up a super fund to trust deed upgrades, online portfolio administration and financial and structural planning. It also offers free seminars on whether an SMSF is right for you. For more information visit www.superconcepts.com.au.

Getting serious about SMSFs

SMSFs are regulated by the Australian Taxation Office, which has rules on how SMSFs must be established, structured, audited, managed and administered. These rules are outlined in the *Superannuation Industry (Supervision) Act 1993* (the *SIS Act*) — the guiding legislation for the superannuation industry. Contravening the *SIS* legislation evokes penalties, so your obligations as a trustee are both serious and potentially financial.

To establish an SMSF you must satisfy the following:

- It has four or fewer members.
- No member of the fund is an employee of another member of the fund unless they are related.
- Each member is a trustee.
- No trustee of the fund receives any remuneration for their services as a trustee.

An SMSF can have a company as a trustee, provided the fund has four or fewer members and that each member of the fund is a director of the company.

Further, that no member is an employee of another member (unless they are related), and the corporate trustee does not receive any remuneration for its services as a trustee.

Anyone who is over 18 years of age, has no criminal record, not bankrupt or insolvent, has not been disqualified by a regulator or subject to a civil penalty order under the *SIS Act*, can be a trustee. Trustees ensure the fund is managed correctly and that it complies with legislation.

Visit the Australian Taxation Office website at www.ato.gov.au to get a copy of its useful guide entitled 'DIY Super ... It's your money, but not yet!'

Making a cost comparison

What is the point of managing your own SMSF if the costs of doing so make it more expensive than other available superannuation vehicles? Estimates on how much it costs to run your own SMSF start from about $1000 a year, with most of this money absorbed in costs associated with auditing and regular reporting obligations. And if you choose to use additional services, such as an administration vehicle or a wrap account which will do the consolidated reporting for you, the annual cost of having your SMSF will be higher.

Due to the costs associated with managing your own SMSF, professionals in the financial services industry advise investors to have at least $200,000 in superannuation before considering establishing a SMSF, although we think it can be quite cost-effective at the $100,000 mark. The total sum will be reduced on an individual basis if you choose to have the maximum of four members.

While on paper there certainly are more cost-effective superannuation vehicles available in the market, this becomes negligible if the investment returns and tax efficiency that can be gained from an SMSF are favourable for your personal circumstances.

Getting help

DIY investing is exactly that, but you will need some advice along the way, particularly in establishing an SMSF, as well as other advice to make sure the investment strategy of the fund is in line with the goals of the trustees. You should look for advice on registration requirements, strategy, administration and reporting, auditing and calculating allocated pensions.

Establishment and trust deeds

To register an SMSF, a trust must be established with trustees, property, identifiable beneficiaries and the intent to create a trust. A trust deed must also be established outlining the rules of the fund and the funds' objectives. An accountant or solicitor can help you with the trust deed.

To receive concessional tax treatment, trustees must complete an application known as an 'Application to Register for the New Tax System Superannuation Entity' and send it to the Australian Taxation Office. Upon receiving this application a Tax File Number and an Australian Business Number will be issued.

Investment strategy

An experienced, non-conflicted financial adviser might have a couple of roles to play with regard to SMSFs.

First, they are a source of advice on whether an SMSF is a viable option for you. Second, an independent financial planner can help structure your investments to help realise your fund's investment objectives. Their knowledge of investments and products will help streamline the process of sorting through the plethora of products on the market and to develop a long-term investment strategy that will give your SMSF direction.

Perhaps more importantly, a licensed financial planner is the only professional allowed to give such advice under Australia's financial services regulations. An accountant who does not hold an Australian Financial Services Licence can only advise on the establishment, operation, structuring and valuation of an SMSF, not on investment strategy.

Finally, there are some legislative limitations on what can and cannot be held legitimately as assets within an SMSF. These rules are designed to ensure investment decisions are motivated only by the desire of generating investment returns for members. This is known as the Sole Purpose Test and is part of the *SIS Act*.

Professional advice will help guide you through this maze. As your needs and your members' needs change, advisers can help adapt the investment strategy to your new objectives. In this way, the role of a financial planner is ongoing.

Administration and reporting

This is probably the factor investors most commonly gloss over when deciding to set up an SMSF: the ongoing administration and reporting associated with the fund.

The record-keeping alone for a SMSF is fairly full-on. Under law, the trustees of SMSFs must, among other things:

- Keep accurate and accessible accounting records that explain the transactions and financial position of the fund for a minimum of five years.
- Prepare an annual operating statement and an annual statement of the fund's financial position and keep these records for a minimum of five years.
- Prepare minutes of trustee meetings (where matters affecting the fund were discussed), and prepare records of all changes of trustees and members' written consent to be appointed as trustees. Each of these documents must be kept for a minimum of ten years.
- Keep copies of all annual returns lodged for a minimum of five years.
- Keep copies of all reports given to members for a minimum of ten years.

Auditing

This is an annual commitment and must be conducted by an approved auditor, who must provide a report to the trustees stating that the fund has been audited.

The fund's financial health and compliance are covered in this report, and if the auditor is not satisfied with the action taken by trustees to fix any problems they have with the fund, they will notify the ATO.

Allocated pensions

An allocated pension enables an individual to invest a lump sum and to draw down an annual pension over their lifetime. If an allocated pension is paid by an SMSF to its members, quite complex calculations are required to make sure payments are correct.

The pension payment made is based on calculations that make sure that payments are no less than the minimum and no more than the maximum calculated in accordance with Schedules 1A or 1AAB of the Superannuation Industry (Supervision) Regulations 1994 (SISR). These schedules are used to calculate the limits for each year based on the pension account balance at 1 July.

To actually calculate these limits, the pension account balance is divided by each of the maximum and the minimum pension valuation factors in the schedule according to the pension recipient's age.

Chapter 10

PROPERTY ADVICE

Australians have such affection for property investments that we believe property, unlike other asset classes, deserves its own chapter in this book. Unfortunately this sector is riddled with scams and advice is more unreliable than in any other area.

As we have said, good advice is critical. But where can you get property advice and who is licensed to provide it?

Since the 1980s, rising property prices in Australia have enabled many investors to leverage the value in their own home, using the capital gain and equity to invest in other property. As a result, more investors than ever before are involved in the property sector.

That means the need for property advice has really grown, both out of the demand for advice and the lack of representation for the property buyer. As we all know, although real estate agents liaise with buyers and sellers, they generally work on behalf of sellers, leaving buyers to their own devices. The main source of advice for buyers and investors these days is from buyers' agents, who operate under a normal real estate agent's licence, but on behalf of the buyer.

Adding another layer of complexity to the property market is the range of products on offer beyond direct property. Indirect property investments such as managed funds and listed property trusts spread across the sub-classes of property, including residential, commercial and industrial property, add to the range of investment options on offer. Both of these factors have facilitated a huge growth in the property advice sector, which now offers a range of services.

Yet despite our demand and need for good property advice, it remains one of the most unregulated and under-regulated areas of the Australian financial services industry. To put it simply, unlike other areas of the industry such as financial planning or stockbroking, you do not need to be licensed to provide property advice. Furthermore, if you do have a complaint about the services you have received, there is really no clear recourse for action. We'll talk more about both of these issues later.

Since 2004, the Australian financial services industry has operated under the full implementation of the *Financial Services Reform Act 2001* (*FSRA*), legislation designed to bring all financial services and products under one regulatory regime. However, *FSRA* does not apply to real estate agents in the capacity of selling individual property. The Real Estate Institute of Australia (REIA), the peak real estate body in Australia that represents about 80 per cent of real estate businesses, explains this further:

> *The Australian Securities & Investments Commission has advised the REIA that while advice in relation to investment property is not covered by the* FSRA, *if agents compare the potential return on such properties to other financial products like shares or managed investments they may be caught as they may be regarded as providing financial product advice in relation to shares and managed funds ...*
>
> *Agents providing these services will either need to be licensed or authorised by a licensee and must also meet all requirements of ASIC Policy Statement 146.*

Despite this surprising regulatory approach — or rather lack of one — the property advice industry has received increased attention from a variety of regulatory bodies concerned about the growing number of property scams appearing in Australia.

As a result, in December 2004, the Parliamentary Joint Committee on Corporate and Financial Services resolved to look into the effectiveness of the regulation of property investment advice. In February 2005, the Law Institute of Victoria (LIV) provided a submission to the Parliamentary Joint Committee in which it observed the 'current deficiency existing in regulation of an aggressive property promotion industry'.

It stated: 'This deficiency is evidenced by the numerous property investor schemes that continue to flourish with little consumer recourse available.' In June 2005, the Committee issued its findings in a report titled 'Property Investment Advice — Safe as houses?' The report found significant problems with the provision of property investment advice as well as wealth-creation training services. In particular:

- the variable quality of advice services
- the lack of disclosure of commissions and arrangements, as well as the relationship between promoters and property developers
- consumers lack of opportunity to have their questions answered and consider a property investment
- misrepresentations that property investments are risk-free or low risk
- difficulties consumers experience in receiving promised refunds on seminars and courses or in taking action against a provider.

Such findings are a sobering reminder to all investors of the dangers of accepting property advice as well as the current lack of regulation and protection for consumers.

The report concluded:

> *Given the public's obvious appetite for property investments, the Committee would ideally like to see the situation where all investment advisers, including financial planners, can provide professional advice on all asset classes including retail property. Until that ideal situation is achieved, there is obviously a need for a much better-organised and properly trained group of advisers who can provide good advice on property investments.*

The regulatory problems of the property investment advice industry are twofold.

First, as we have already noted, there is a lack of regulation of the industry, particularly regulation designed to prevent the development of 'get-rich-quick' property schemes and seminars. But there is also a lack of regulation in fundamental property practices. For example, there is no statutory code of practice that applies to the regulation of auctions in the real estate industry. Some states have their own laws and some state-based Real Estate Institutes have introduced their own guiding principles.

Meanwhile, state-based regulations prevail across a range of property practices and vary across states on practices ranging from dummy bidding to conveyancing. Such an approach creates industry confusion, which leads to the second problem with regulation.

According to the LIV, there is significant crossover of jurisdiction between ASIC, the Australian Competition & Consumer Commission and state-based consumer affairs departments. There doesn't seem to be a consensus on whether it would be better to have a common or state-based approach to prevent this. The result of such a system means good legal advice becomes critical if you need to navigate your way through the industry.

A positive development for the industry has been REIA's establishment in August 2006 of its Fundamental Principles of Conduct, which were designed to promote and encourage 'a high standard of ethical practice' by its members.

It is amazing to think these principles never existed before 2006! The document states that REIA members should:

- hold the required professional qualifications, insurances and indemnities necessary to operate within their state or territory
- maintain and improve their knowledge, skills and qualifications over the course of their careers
- have a working knowledge and act in accordance with the relevant laws governing the real estate profession, including codes of conduct and the rules of professional associations
- act in the best interests of their client and in accordance with their instructions, except where to do so is unlawful or contrary to good agency practice
- act ethically, fairly and honestly when dealing with all parties and will not allow any person to believe that they are acting for any party other than their client
- treat fellow real estate practitioners with respect and professional courtesy — members shall disclose their role to all other agents involved in a property transaction
- not use or disclose any confidential or sensitive information obtained while acting on behalf of a client or dealing with a customer, except where required by law to disclose [information]
- endeavour to prevent or resolve disputes with a view to minimising the number of complaints made against the real estate practitioner. Members will inform all

complainants of the alternate avenues of complaint open to them
- disseminate relevant information received from, or required by, the REIA (or state institutes) where this will assist the ongoing development of the profession.
Members shall actively seek to continually improve the status and general operation of the real estate profession for the benefit of clients and consumers.

Source: REIA

Who is licensed to provide property advice?

Real estate agents who provide advice only on direct property investments and associated financing arrangements are licensed through state and territory agencies. They are subject to the *Trade Practices Act 1974* prohibitions covering such behaviour as unconscionable conduct, misleading and deceptive conduct and false and misleading conduct.

There are real estate agents who offer more than just property advice, including advice on financial products such as insurance, geared investments or property investments structured as managed investments. These agents are licensed by ASIC or are employees or authorised representatives of a licence holder and they come under the Corporations Law.

A speech given by ASIC Commissioner Professor Berna Collier in May 2004 highlights the bizarre licensing situation:

People who confine themselves to advising on and promoting direct investment in property are not required:
- to meet training and competency requirements
- to disclose their conflicts of interest to those they advise

- to belong to, or be an authorised representative of a licensee that belongs to, an approved external dispute resolution scheme
- to meet the many requirements of the Australian Financial Services Licence and the other requirements of Chapter 7 of the *Corporations Act.*

Source: 'ASIC and the property sector', a presentation to the 2004 Listed Property Trust Leaders Summit given by Professor Berna Collier, ASIC Commissioner, 18 May 2004.

Finding good property advice

One of the most important points about property advice is that it can be expensive. Whether it is conveyancing fees, legal costs or straight property investment advice, all these services cost money and trying to scrimp on costs can be a real downfall for many investors when approaching this asset class.

Areas where some investors try and save include conveyancing fees, auction costs and by managing investment properties themselves. And although it is important to be wary of the costs involved with all these aspects of advice, make sure the onus is on good advice, not free advice.

It is interesting to note that often the scams where investors lose thousands of dollars within the property industry include the provision of 'free' advice via seminars. This is how they get people to come and listen to their promises of amazing and guaranteed high returns. Don't get sucked in!

Some seminars are usually overpriced and poor value for money, and their organisers often make misleading or deceptive claims, push strategies that could be financially dangerous and promote outright scams.

The Parliamentary Joint Committee on Corporate and Financial Services received the following information from various submissions on how property spruikers operate.

- Often seminars are pitched as educational seminars rather than financial advice, to avoid regulatory requirements around the provision of financial advice. They say they are promoting strategy rather than advice.
- High-pressure and high emerging selling techniques are used in order to rush consumers into a decision.
- Those that do promote specific investment opportunities often get commissions to do so, creating an obvious conflict of interest that is not disclosed.

Buying property off the plan can also involve the provision of a lot of information for free. The message here is that it is important to keep your wits about you and to make the distinction between what is information and what is advice. A true independent property adviser will charge you a fee, so the first rule of thumb when it comes to getting good property advice is the same as for all financial advice: there is no such thing as free advice.

So why has property in particular been prone to investment scams? It's undoubtedly largely because of the lax regulations covering property. There is little doubt that the real estate boom has made unsophisticated investors forget their caution so that property has become an attractive domain for unscrupulous operators looking to take advantage of individuals' greed. This situation is likely to continue, given the tight rental market. More property developments will spring up, with promoters looking for investors to provide the equity, and this means that much more needs to be done to regulate the industry.

A recent examples of a property scam is Westpoint. The collapse of the Westpoint property development scheme in Perth was a scandal that cost thousands of Australians their life savings. Some people invested through licensed financial planners, while others invested through someone they thought was licensed or responded directly to newspaper advertisements and seminars.

It is far better to use a licensed adviser because they have clear responsibilities to know the product and know their client. There is also recourse for investors if they do get into trouble.

From a regulatory point of view, the realm of property investment advice is not well defined. With the exception of Queensland, which has some specific laws relating to property marketers, property advisers are principally regulated by general consumer protection laws at a state and federal level. Real estate is not regarded as a financial product and so is not part of the *Financial Services Reform Act 2001*.

So at this point in the development of the property advice industry, it is a case of buyer beware. The Eureka Report's property editor Monique Wakelin, who (with her husband Richard) wrote *Streets Ahead: How to make money from residential property*, says it is crucial to know the right questions to ask of those who claim to provide property advice. This is particularly the case given the lack of training available for the specialist qualifications needed to provide quality property investment advice.

According to the Wakelins, you should ask the following questions of an adviser you are considering to help ascertain their experience, possible conflicts of interest, remuneration structure and ultimately whether they will provide the service you want and value for money:

- How much experience do you have in advising purchasers on property acquisition?
- How much experience do you have in advising purchasers on direct residential property?
- Are you and your company licensed?
- What formal qualifications do you and your staff hold?

- Do you have unrestricted access to the property market?
- How are you and your company remunerated?
- What research is your advice based on?
- What ongoing professional education do your directors and advisers undertake?
- What ongoing services can your company offer after I've made a purchase?
- How will you make yourself accountable to me as a client?

> *Source:* Streets Ahead: How to make money from residential property, *Monique and Richard Wakelin, 2002.*

Why bother with property?

Given the problems associated with sourcing good property advice, why should investors bother with property investing? Well, the excellent long-term investment performance of property is difficult to ignore, and a lot of investors simply prefer the perceived safety of property — the fact it's an investment you can actually walk around in and touch, unlike shares and so on. It is also possible to borrow more against property than other investments, and therefore gear your returns more.

The ASX Investment Performance Report conducted by the Russell Investment Group found that over a ten-year period to 31 December 2005, Australian shares, listed property and residential property were the three top-performing asset classes at the top and lowest marginal tax rates.

That is, the after-tax returns of listed property ranged between 10.4 and 12.6 per cent a year at both tax rates, while Australian shares returned between 9.2 and 11.7 per cent a year over the same period.

Over a 20-year period, and depending on marginal tax brackets, returns for Australian shares ranged between 10.4 and 12.4 per cent a year. This was followed by listed property with returns ranging between 9.7 and 11.8 per cent a year and residential investment property with returns between 8.9 and 10.9 per cent a year.

While long-term investment data is a useful guide to investment performance, it does not guarantee future performance. It is important to remember that different time periods can be used to demonstrate the cyclical nature of any asset class, even property. For example, during the 1990s, the best-performing asset class in the ten-year periods up to 1991, 1992, 1993, 1994 and 1998, 1999, 2000 and 2001 was international shares.

As mentioned earlier, there is a growing range of property options for investors, ranging from direct to indirect property, and these in turn will attract different rates of return. For example, according to the ASX, most listed property trusts yield between 6 and 10 per cent a year in commercial property and only 2.5–5 per cent in direct residential property.

Other factors

Investing in property provides your portfolio with what is known as an inflation hedge; that is, an investment whose value is expected to rise in times of inflation. There are two factors at work here. First, because you are investing in a tangible asset that has a permanent intrinsic value, the nominal price can be expected to rise in line with the reduction in the purchasing power of money resulting from inflation.

The second factor is the scarcity factor of the land content. Even in a large and lightly populated country such as Australia there is a scarcity of land where people want to live and work (in city and metropolitan areas and on the coastal fringe). As our population increases the scarcity factor will tend to propel the value of well-positioned land at a more rapid rate than the inflation factor alone.

The ability to use gearing as an investment tool makes property particularly unique and attractive. Gearing effectively means borrowing to invest. It gives you greater buying power and opportunity to build your wealth and can even lower your tax liability.

Positive gearing means the income derived from an investment exceeds the cost of borrowing. Negative gearing is effectively the opposite; that is, the income derived from an investment does not cover the costs of borrowing. This might not sound like a good thing, but under Australian tax law you can, in many instances, claim for the loss and use it to offset other taxable income, such as your salary.

Of course, there is a flip side to such benefits. The conditions that apply when you take out a loan to invest may not stay the same. If interest rates rise, meeting repayments can become difficult. Or the investment may not make the return you desire or need to keep the conditions for gearing optimal.

Aspects of property investing

While Australians love the tangible nature of property investing, this characteristic can also be a downside. That's because selling property is not the easiest or quickest thing to do, and transaction costs can be high (for both sellers and buyers). This is why many investors are attracted to listed property trusts (LPTs).

Listed property trusts
According to the ASX, there are advantages of buying and selling LPTs including:

- easy and immediate access to the LPT of your choice as purchases and sales are done during normal ASX trading hours
- flexibility to use 'limit orders' to buy and sell at prices you specify

- information on your investments is easily accessible in newspapers and websites
- transactions are settled in three days
- if your transaction or holding is subject to fraud or insolvency of your licensed adviser, the National Guarantee Fund may cover your losses
- LPTs are subject to supervision through initial and ongoing ASX requirements.

Because LPTs are listed on the market, units can be bought and sold in a matter of hours. However, they are also more volatile and prices tend to fluctuate with market movements. Meanwhile, unlisted property trusts and syndicates are less liquid.

Property can also be a difficult asset class in which to achieve diversification. This is why it is beneficial to make the most of the range of property vehicles available in the market: listed and unlisted property trusts, property syndicates and direct property.

Within property there is residential, commercial and industry property, which covers a range of property types such as shopping centres, factories and hotels. By investing through an LPT, you can gain access to a range of sub-sectors within the asset class. Also, these vehicles are professionally managed, so you don't have to worry about selecting the property or managing the costs associated with the fund.

Unlisted property trusts and syndicates tend not to offer the same level of diversification because they are smaller than LPTs. Part of the income distributed from both listed and unlisted property trusts can be tax-deferred.

Managing your investments
Another important factor to consider with property investing is how you will manage your investments. Direct

property investments are either managed by yourself or through a real estate agent, who typically charges a 5 per cent annual management fee (or more). Listed and unlisted property trusts are professionally managed and these enable you to outsource the investment decisions associated with the product. This, of course, comes at a cost.

Annual management fees on LPTs range up to 1 per cent a year. Fees are higher in unlisted trusts and property syndicates because of the smaller economies of scale afforded by their size.

Unlisted trusts and syndicates also have an up-front charge (which may not be immediately obvious) to enable the manager to pay commissions to financial advisers. You also need to watch management charges on property purchases and sales, and investigate what costs you would incur if you need to access your funds before the nominated termination date.

On the subject of costs, it is important to make a full inventory of all the costs associated with your property investment, particularly direct property investing. Government charges can really add up, so make sure you know what your net costs are when considering direct and indirect property investments.

Stamp duty is state legislated tax and it is the largest initial cost of buying a property, apart from the initial deposit. Each state has a different stamp duty level. State government land tax may also be payable on the unimproved value of land, with the principal place of residence being exempt. You should check what rules apply in your state before making any property investment. Council rates and utilities, including water, electricity and gas, are also worth remembering as these are the real day-to-day costs of investing in direct property.

Chapter 11

HALF-TRUTHS, FLAWED THINKING AND MISREPRESENTATIONS

This chapter looks at some of the strategies and ideas pushed by the financial planning industry that might be more in the interests of financial planners than you the investor. This is not to say that there is not some truth behind the strategies and wisdom, just that this truth is sometimes distorted to suit the agenda of the financial services industry.

Gearing

Gearing — that is borrowing money to invest — is a legitimate personal investment strategy. By borrowing money to invest you increase the expected return of your investment portfolio, and you increase the volatility (fluctuations in value) of your portfolio.

The last point is important: by borrowing to invest you *increase the volatility and risk* of your investment portfolio. That means that gearing is a strategy only suited to those investors with a high tolerance for fluctuations in the value of their portfolio.

Let's think about how gearing works for a financial planner. If a client comes to see a planner with $50,000 to invest, a commission-based financial planner is likely to point them towards a managed fund. The managed fund will pay the planner a trailing commission. In this case, let's say the trailing commission is worth 0.5 per cent of the value of the investment. That is $250 a year, every year, of income for the financial planner.

The financial planner might say to the investor, 'Why don't you borrow to invest and increase your exposure to the market? You could borrow another $50,000, add it to the $50,000 that you already have, and suddenly you have $100,000 of exposure to the market.'

The financial planner organises the $50,000 margin loan (a kind of investment loan) for the client. The gearing strategy means that now the financial planner is earning a trailing commission of $500 a year on a $100,000 managed fund investment. They will also earn a trailing commission on the margin loan, so they are earning another $250 a year in trailing commissions. If investment returns are strong, the gearing strategy will work well for the client. Regardless of investment returns, the gearing strategy will work well for the financial planner, who has trebled their trailing commission from $250 to $750.

Gearing is a legitimate investment strategy, but it is one that only suits aggressive investors who are comfortable with volatility and who have a particularly long investment time frame. It should come with the clear warning that:

- It is not for everybody.
- Gearing means that the underlying volatility of an investment is increased.
- Gearing means that there will be much greater losses of capital in the event of severe market downturns, which do happen from time to time.

It is a particularly risky strategy in an investment environment where interest rates are rising sharply and investment values are falling sharply.

Where a commission-based financial planner is recommending the strategy, there should be a warning that this is a particularly lucrative strategy for them.

Life insurance

Those clients of the financial services industry who are younger — say 40 or less — tend to be categorised as 'wealth accumulators'. That is a green light for financial planners to focus on two strategies (which may be more in the interests of the adviser than the client):

- Make sure that the client has plenty of life insurance.
- Use a gearing strategy for the client.

We discussed gearing in the previous section, which allows a financial planner to increase their commission payments through encouraging the client to borrow money to invest. The other way a commission-based financial planner can build an income stream from a young client is to sell them an array of life insurance products.

Before proceeding any further it is crucial to emphasise that life insurance is an important part of any person's financial plan. We are certainly not suggesting it is an area that should be ignored. But we are suggesting that it is an area that might be subject to over-zealous recommendation by financial planners.

That's because life insurance pays very generously to commission-based financial planners. The commission tends to average about 30 per cent of each year's premiums. The more insurance a financial planner can recommend to you, the better off their commission-based income stream becomes.

And here lies the first problem. Is the financial planner recommending an ever-increasing array of life insurance products with increasing levels of cover because it is best for you and your family, or best for them? After visiting a financial planner many clients find themselves with a level of insurance cover that means they and their family would be in a better financial position if they were permanently disabled or killed.

The second problem is that some of the cheapest life insurance available, through group life policies in superannuation funds, is often ignored by financial planners because it does not pay any commissions. Most superannuation funds can offer a good base of relatively low-cost death and total and permanent disability (TPD) cover, and income protection insurance that pays a benefit for two years. A person could add trauma insurance and income protection insurance that pays a benefit through to age 65 after a waiting period of two years and end up with a nice complete insurance plan, much of which would be low-cost group cover held in superannuation. With the growth of superannuation choice and superannuation portability, an innovative financial planner can help build good insurance solutions around low-cost insurance offered through superannuation.

These two problems are exacerbated because life insurance is such an emotive issue. Take death cover, for instance. For young parents, it is very easy for a financial planner to encourage the parents to take more than they think is necessary, because a higher level of cover means a better quality of life for the children if both parents should die. This is emotional stuff. Just keep in mind that the commission-based financial planner is not only driven by a civic-minded desire to see your children thrive in the event of your tragic demise — they might be driven by the commissions as well.

The best strategy is to think through, and discuss with the important people in the situation, what you would like to happen financially if you were to die suddenly or be permanently disabled, and to then put these arrangements in place.

Managed funds and wraps

This book has dedicated whole chapters to discussion of managed funds and wraps. Our conclusion is that there is a place for both of them, but for some consumers they are not the universal investment solution that commission-based financial planners would have you believe.

The 'half-truth' here is the overstatement of value that managed funds and wraps provide. There is much greater detail on both of these topics in the relevant chapters in the book.

Time in the market or timing?

You often hear that it is 'time in the market' that counts, not market timing. If this is the case, then there is never a bad time to invest! All you have to do is invest now, and hold on for five to seven years, the time frame most commonly promoted for an investment in a growth asset class, and everything will be OK. This oft-promoted idea — that provided you hold an investment in a growth asset class for at least five to seven years you cannot go wrong — suits a financial planner who makes money from managed fund commissions.

Austin Donnelly is an investment adviser with nearly 50 years' experience. In his book *Good Advice — A Guide for Investors and Advisers* (Wrightbooks, 1998), he strongly critisises what he refers to as the 'don't-you-worry-about-that' syndrome, which says that 'provided you stay in the market for three to five years, all will be well'. He argues that reliable advice should point to slumps in investment markets causing losses of up to 40 per cent and more, with up to ten years needed for recovery. There have been periods of 15 years in which the All-Ordinaries index, which measures the performance of Australian shares, has achieved no sustained net gain.

Consider more recent investment returns which, to the end of December 2006, have seen poor returns from international investments — not much better than an average return of 1 per cent a year over the past five years. The 'time in the market' wisdom of being invested for five years has not really helped investors in this asset class. This in turn must be discouraging for investors who started by thinking that in five years' time their investment would be sailing along.

There is certainly some truth in the saying that it is time in the market that counts — that investing for the long term makes sense — just as there is wisdom in the advice not to try *and* time markets. The misrepresentation occurs when the saying is used to suggest that:

- There is never a bad time to invest — a great strategy if you are in the business of selling managed funds!
- If you invest for a five-year period everything will be OK. This is not true; plenty of five-year periods have produced discouraging investment returns.

The problem with this half-truth is that investors are entitled to, but not told, the full truth; they are told a half-truth that suits the commission-based salesmen. What might be the cost of this half truth? Investors go and invest their money without fully understanding that investing requires patience beyond five years and that they should expect times of poor returns as well as times of good returns. As soon as returns start to fall below their unrealistic expectations, the disappointment means that they sell out of their investments, only buying back in once their mood changes after seeing markets perform extremely well. They are effectively selling low and buying high because they were not initially told the full truth about how investment markets work. So, does this problem exist in reality?

A famous study by Dalbar Incorporated looked at the actual returns US investors had received from investing in managed funds, taking into account both managed fund returns and the trading behaviour of the investors (that is, when they bought and sold). The average return from the sharemarket investment index in the US over the period from 1985 to 2006 was a return of 11.90 per cent a year. The managed fund investors, however, made a return of only 3.90 per cent a year over this period because their behaviour in buying and selling managed funds was extremely poorly timed. Perhaps, if their professional advisers had given them more realistic information about market returns, they would have been more patient and received much strong investment returns.

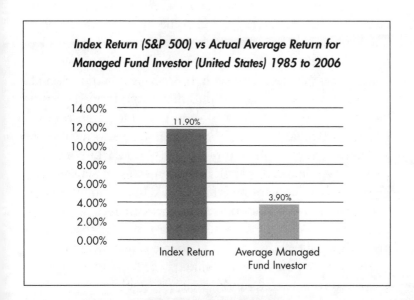

Assessing performance

This wisdom stands in opposition to the warning that is seen on financial services advertisements, where we are told that past performance is not an indication of future outperformance. However, the industry does not behave as though this is the case.

Consider managed fund advertisements. Most of them advertise above-average historical returns in the hope that investors will assume that these returns will be repeated in the future. Sure, the small print says that past performance is not an indicator of future outperformance, but the big print says the opposite. For past performance to be an indicator of future outperformance, we would need to see persistence in high levels of fund performance. The research cited in Chapter 7, however, showed that this does not exist, that good past performance does not lead to future outperformance.

Investors need to keep in mind that there are many thousands of managed funds in the Australian investment landscape. In any given period some of them are going to outperform just based on luck, not because of the skill of fund managers.

Financial planners can, with 100 per cent certainty, build you a portfolio of managed funds that outperformed over the past five years. There is no skill in that. However, research suggests that the fact that these funds outperformed in the past means nothing for future long-term outperformance.

When a financial planner recommends managed fund investments by using past performance data, the implication is that this data is relevant to its future performance. More than this, the research companies' use of past performance implies predictive value in this, which of course is not accurate.

Think about this for a minute: if past performance did lead to future performance, then we would not need any financial advisers at all to choose investments. All we would need would be a table showing historical managed fund performance and we could pick the highest-performing managed funds from that.

Percentage fees

The standard for charging fees in the financial services industry is to charge a fee as a percentage. Managed funds charge their management fees as a percentage. Wraps and platforms charge their fees as a percentage. The majority of financial planners charge their fees as a percentage. Commissions paid to financial planners from insurances are also calculated in percentage terms.

The problem with this system of charging is that it disguises the actual dollar amount being charged in fees. A 2 per cent fee on a portfolio of $100,000 doesn't sound like an unreasonable fee; a $2000 cash fee sounds much more significant.

Consider how a fee affects the returns. Historical investment returns from growth assets have been about 12 per cent. Returns from defensive fixed-interest and cash investments are currently about 6.5 per cent. A balanced portfolio with 60 per cent in growth assets and 40 per cent in defensive assets has an expected return of 9.8 per cent. A 2 per cent fee erodes more than one-fifth of the expected return from the balanced portfolio!

The insidious nature of percentage fees is such that you can face a few layers of fees without understanding how much is being paid. Add a moderate-sounding wrap fee to a moderate-sounding managed fund fee to a moderate-sounding financial planner fee and pretty soon your portfolio returns are groaning under the combined weight of all these 'moderate' fees.

Part of the reason we accept these high fees lies in the previous section on past investment performance; that is, we assume that the financial planner organising our portfolio has the skill to pick investments that will provide a higher-than-average return because of their strong historical performance. So, we say to ourselves, 'Why bother worrying about fees when our portfolio returns are going to be above average, anyway?'

Of course, percentage-based fees work extremely well for the financial services industry. Consider an average superannuation fund. Over the course of a year it grows through investment returns and additional contributions. Assuming a balanced fund with investment returns of 9.8 per cent, less 2 per cent in fees, which comes to 7.8 per cent after fees. That return alone increases fees to the financial services industry by 7.8 per cent a year — about three times the rate of inflation. Add to that the additional superannuation contributions being received from the fund and you can see how well percentage-based fees work for the financial services industry.

In December 2006 the combined superannuation wealth of Australians was reported to pass the $1 billion mark. If we assume that the average fee for superannuation investments is 1 per cent, and it may well be a lot higher than that, the fees from superannuation investments collected by the financial services industry total $10 billion a year, or about $500 for every man, woman and child in Australia. That doesn't include the fees from non-superannuation investments, wraps, insurances and so on.

Setting your financial direction

Contrary to what most people in the financial services industry would have you believe, the basics of setting your own financial direction and building wealth over time are not complicated.

You need to spend less than you earn, invest the difference regularly in growth assets (such as a mix of Australian shares, listed property and international shares) and patiently wait for investment returns.

You need to think about how you and your family would cope in the case of death or loss of the ability to earn income, and put in place estate planning and insurance arrangements to help cope financially with such an eventuality.

You need to make good use of the superannuation environment, which allows tax-effective contributions, a low tax rate on investment earnings and tax-free withdrawals after the age of 60.

This is not to say that a good financial planner will not be helpful in achieving your financial goals, just that if you choose to take a self-directed path, the fundamentals of creating wealth over time are not as difficult as the financial services industry sometimes makes it sound.

The conflicts of interest within the financial services industry lead to a complicated network of 'semi-wisdom', strategies and advice that could be characterised as being somewhat deceptive. Keeping this in mind will help anyone who encounters it to assess its merits for themselves.

A final word

ASIC's advice that if you don't understand a financial product, stay away, should apply to all your investment decisions. ASIC recommends the following questions when deciding on a financial product:

1   How does this product work? Use the Product Disclosure
    Statement to find out:
    – how your money will be invested
    – how the product will generate returns
    – how these will be paid to you.
2   Could you get your money back out of this product if you
    need to, and are there any fees if you exit early?

3   Is there a ready market for you to sell your product to another party?

4   Can you describe to a friend or partner how this product works?

5   Have you got enough information to understand the product and the associated risks?

6   Are you comfortable with the product issuer? Does the issuer have a sound business reputation?

7   Did the product issuer approach you, and if so, why?

8   What are the risks?

9   What risks do products like this generally involve?

10   Are there any extra risks involved with this product?

11   How could your investment be affected by a major shift in the economy and market sentiment?

12   How could rising interest rates affect you, particularly if you've borrowed money to invest?

13   Have you considered operational risks such as fraud, company failure or systems failure?

14   Does the product suit your needs?

15   How much knowledge and experience do you have as an investor?

16   Have you compared the product with other investment options?

17   What could you lose and could you afford it? What are the potential losses?

18   Are you investing funds you may need in retirement?

19   Are you borrowing to invest? Will you still be able to repay the loan if your investment performs badly?

20   Are you putting your home at risk if the investment fails?

21   Have you obtained professional financial advice?

Source: www.fido.asic.gov.au

INDEX